In Search of Healing

IN SEARCH OF HEALING

Whole-Body Healing Through
the Mind-Body-Spirit Connection

William A. McGarey, M.D.

A PERIGEE BOOK

A Perigee Book
Published by The Berkley Publishing Group
200 Madison Avenue
New York, NY 10016

First edition: April 1996

Published simultaneously in Canada.

The Putnam Berkley World Wide Web site address is
http://www.berkley.com

Library of Congress Cataloging-in-Publication Data

McGarey, William A.
    In search of healing : whole-body healing through the
mind-body-spirit connection / William A. McGarey.
        p.   cm.
    "A Perigee book".
    ISBN 0-399-51989-0
    1. Mental healing. 2. Spiritual healing. 3. Holistic medicine.
I. Title.
RZ400.M36 1996
615.5—dc20   95-24040

Printed in the United States of America

10 9 8 7 6 5 4 3 2 1

Contents

INTRODUCTION   xi

PART ONE   THE MIND

1. Understanding the Wholeness of Man   3
2. Defining Our Life's Journey   8
3. Understanding Illness   17
4. Holistic Medicine in Action   26
5. The Mind in Control   37
6. The Conscious and Unconscious Mind   48
7. The Power of Choice   56
8. Your Seven Spiritual Centers   64

PART TWO   THE BODY

9. Harnessing Energy   81
10. Physiology and Healing   99
11. Healthful Diet and the Creative Life Force   124
12. Healing, Regeneration, and Longevity   132

PART THREE   THE SPIRIT

13. The Soul's Journey   151
14. Understanding Our Spiritual Nature   164

15. Faith and Illness   173
16. Tapping into Our Spiritual Energy   189
17. The Keys to Well-Being   209

CONCLUSION   In Search of Healing   229

Suggested Reading   233

All Biblical quotations are taken from the New English Bible or the Authorized King James Version.

At the Association for Research and Enlightenment in Virginia Beach, Virginia, where Edgar Cayce's work has been preserved, each "reading" has been given a number representing the individual who asked for the reading. These numbers appear at the end of the quotations used throughout.

*. . . for the time has arisen in the earth
when men everywhere seek to know more
of the mysteries of the mind, the soul, the
soul's mind which man recognizes as existent . . .*
    —254-52 of the Cayce readings

Introduction

I didn't realize when I took a coffee break with Dr. Bill Rogers between seeing patients at the Maricopa County Hospital outpatient department back in 1955 that this meeting would be instrumental in changing my life.

But it happened, and it was strange the way it went. We simply started talking about our hobbies.

Bill said his interests were in nutrition and religion. I thought that was strange. But then I did a rerun on my life back in Ohio before I was "invited" by the President to take another stint in the service of my country. (That letter led me into the U.S.A.F. as a flight surgeon for two years and allowed me to relocate in Arizona from my hometown of Wellsville, Ohio.)

When I got to thinking about my first five years in the practice of general medicine in Wellsville, and my college and medical school years prior to that, I began to realize that nutrition and religion were not such strange bedfellows in my own experience. And I shared that with Bill as we drank coffee.

Religion was not an unknown force in my life. I was planning on entering the ministry in the Presbyterian Church during my first two years in college, but then changed to pre-med half the way through. Although I did not follow my first choice for a profession, I retained my deep beliefs in God, although I could not understand the significance of the world we live in. That was a puzzle for me. But religion as a hobby—yes, I could grasp that.

Nutrition was also no stranger to my experience. I found it to be helpful to me in my early practice of medicine. So Bill's ideas and mine seemed to interlock. I found our relationship building on a solid foundation, and we really began our conversations.

The next Tuesday evening, instead of attending the County Society medical meeting inside Good Samaritan Hospital, Bill and I spent the time inside his car in the parking lot, talking about his philosophy. It seemed he understood reincarnation to be totally a valid concept. For me, it was new and strange, but I instantly recognized how it substantiated so many aspects of my religious beliefs. That got us started on a voyage of reading and experiencing events in the field of parapsychology.

We also "discovered" Milton Erickson, a famous medical hypnotherapist, and became his students for a while. We began meeting psychics and came to understand that life exists in large measure outside of what I had formerly considered to be the norm.

It wasn't long before I met Hugh Lynn Cayce and was introduced in depth to the Edgar Cayce psychic readings. My life permanently changed, for I knew that I had to work with the Cayce material from then on, for these readings declared that we are truly body, mind, and spirit or soul. And healing the body is not just taking care of a disease. It is dealing with life as the person experiences it, and is interspersed with many lifetimes and always with emotions, attitudes and their byproducts muddying the waters.

Life on Earth is an adventure in consciousness, and illness and healing are a very real and very opportune part of the journey.

So Bill Rogers and that coffee break experience happened as if it had already been planned. And perhaps it really was!

In Search of Healing

The Mind

CHAPTER 1

Understanding the Wholeness of Man

My career in medicine followed a path that led me through interesting experiences that seemed to be much like other physicians'—lots of office patients, hospital visits, home calls, and all those events that build a practice for the average physician.

I was used to the concept that sore throats usually came from strep or staph bacteria that invaded the human body. We didn't think too much about exactly why this happened, or why another patient might be suffering from a stone in the gallbladder or symptoms of angina pectoris. These people had the problems, so we treated them with shots of penicillin or removal of the gallbladder surgically, or perhaps nitroglycerin tablets for the angina. There was much more than that in the practice of medicine in the late forties, of course, and in the fifteen or twenty years that followed the end of World War II.

Basically, however, my skills were developed in diagnosing and then treating my patients who had become ill. And, strangely, it didn't occur to me or my fellow doctors that events in those patients' lives and the emotions that were involved with those events might have had more importance in truly causing the disease than the etiological factors we studied.

My career, then, and my ultimate path in life underwent a

major leap in consciousness and a dramatic turnaround when I discovered the work and readings of a psychic named Edgar Cayce. His suggestions from an unconscious mind that seemed to travel across time and space, more easily than the jets that exceed the speed of sound today, were loaded with concepts that not only excited me, but also upset many of the entrenched views of how the human body works I had been taught years earlier.

Cayce said, for instance, that this body we find ourselves in at the moment is an energy structure and will respond positively or negatively to other energies; that the atoms and cells that make up the body are pure energy and have consciousness of their own.

Cayce would have us believe that the mind builds the health or the illnesses that are part of our experience in this lifetime. And his concept of life includes many incarnations in the earth for all of us. We are living souls, experiencing life on the plane that we call the earth, coming into this dimension from the spiritual, where we had our beginning, and wherein lies our destiny.

Cayce pointed out that our choices rule our lives more than we would ever dare to believe. He lets us know through his readings that prayer and meditation are an integral part of our relationship with the Divine and in the same manner become part of the healing process.

Life, in the Cayce concept of things, is a journey through the Earth, with a purpose always, and with a destiny that means we must come to know ourselves to be ourselves and yet one with God. And healing, he frequently indicated, is a part of that destiny, in a way that is often difficult to understand. The soul is the eternal part of ourselves, so the soul, as well as the mind and the body, is in need of help to reach our goals.

The Cayce perspective and these concepts, which at first glance might seem very strange, upset most of what I had learned in my medical training about the nature of the body, while at the same time enhancing those elements of belief that were part of my earlier life, when I had planned to become a minister in the Presbyterian Church. For Cayce told those for whom he gave readings that their bodies were truly the temples of the Living God, and that it is there that God would meet them. In his readings, he gave substance and greater understanding to the concept that we were created in the image of God, as living souls, given the power of choice with which we could fashion our lives.

Cayce brought my ego down to earth when I realized the truth behind his statements that all healing comes from within, that it is always a divine happening, and there is no illness that cannot be overcome. For I had thought, as I was taught, that I was healing these people who came to me for help.

Called a "seer" by many, Cayce, for more than forty years, regularly lay down on a couch, released his conscious mind to the care of forces we don't easily understand, and gave a discourse from an extended state of consciousness. This came to be called a reading. Nearly fifteen thousand readings were given prior to his death in 1945, and most were recorded. They have provided for thousands of researchers, and just plain "searchers," a rich source of information dealing for the most part with the illnesses of individuals, and how these illnesses might be dispensed with and eliminated.

His readings pointed out the exquisite nature of what we are dealing with when we attempt to bring about healing of the body, as well as what our true nature and relationship is with God. He told one man:

> *In the beginning, when there was the creating, or the calling of individual entities into being, we were made to be the companions with the Father-God.* 1567-2

Cayce drew a picture that spoke of man as an eternal being, originating in a spiritual realm and having his ultimate destiny in that same dimension. In the interim, he passes through many incarnations here in the earth plane, experiencing and learning more—often on an up-and-down course—about why he is here. The idea of loving others, of always being kind, gentle, forgiving, and understanding in one's relationships with others became not only something Cayce taught in his Sunday school classes, and concepts he tried to live in his life, but also an integral part of the plan suggested in his readings for the healing of the body.

In the process of his advising people on how they might achieve healing, he talked about their emotions, their dreams, their lives in the business world. He discussed relationships, nature, politics, education, and a host of other subjects, all apparently involved in what he liked to call "soul growth." Two-thirds of these readings dealt with human beings and their ailments or illnesses, painting a picture of the wholeness of man in the search for healing. This is a good example:

> For it is true that the body mentally, the body physically, should be and is capable of resuscitating and revitalizing itself, if it is raised in spiritual direction for the activities of disturbing conditions in the body.
>
> Hence mind over matter is not to be lightly spoken of, nor is there any disparaging remark to be made as to the body-physical being revivified, rususcitated, spiritualized such that there is no reaction that may not be revivified. 1152-5

Scattered through these readings were intimations of immortality, urgings to make one's direction and activities purposeful, and instructions in how to live the Christ life. These give me—and you—a background of what we might be dealing with in this adventure.

He spoke often about each of us as body, mind, and spirit—a unity. The essence of this, as I now understand it, is that the spirit of God is the life, the mind is the true builder, and the body is the result of what the mind has done with that power we call the spirit. True healing, Cayce often pointed out, is always marked by an awakening process deep within the cells, the atoms, the tissues of our entire being. Without the enlightening, the change, the new awareness, we do not have that movement in consciousness that may be the purpose for which we are experiencing this lifetime.

To understand the Cayce viewpoint on life as a whole is to embark—if you choose—on a spiritual journey in this material world we live in. It changes our lives, for we are urged always to look at things from a different perspective, to have an open mind, without which we cannot grow toward our destiny.

This is a story, then, about you and what could become your adventure in consciousness. For it seems that all of us, at one time or another, have been in search of that elusive quality we call healing. And we are all trying to remember who we are, where we came from, and where we are going. Deep within the inner reaches of our minds is the desire to come to a oneness with that Force which we instinctively know has brought us into being. We have not even recognized our potential as human beings as yet, and certainly have never fully accomplished what we are destined to achieve.

But it's also a story about our innate creativity, the possibility of an awakening that comes about when we become ill, or meet a certain situation or a certain person. The light goes on, suddenly, and we know we are different from what we thought we were before that event.

The very nature of every human being on the earth makes this adventure a possibility for all. It's an inner activity within the consciousness of each person, seeking a closer relationship with the Divine, the God-Force—what we in the Western world call God. But it's a different experience for each of us, for indeed we are all different.

CHAPTER 2

Defining Our Life's Journey

Having spent the greater part of my life helping people achieve a higher state of health, for me a journey such as this involves the understanding of holistic medicine and the experiences and relationships found there. It also reflects itself within my own total being in a gradual, cell by cell, enlightening process. This is an inward journey, but any seeker can find the light by turning within, as in meditation, by determining to find that light, and by using the influences of many past lifetimes as they show up in daily experiences and relationships. For every person we meet can truly help us on our journey.

Sometimes, our journey begins when we hit bottom and wonder what has happened. We can't go anywhere except up. And the climb may be a bit difficult, with the light seeming to be distant and perhaps almost unreachable. Sometimes our journey is thrust upon us by seemingly inexplicable circumstances.

I have worked with groups of individuals in nearly three hundred residential Temple Beautiful programs at the A.R.E. Clinic in Phoenix, Arizona, since 1978. Each program has eight, ten, or twelve participants who are involved in searching for healing at the level of the body, mind, and spirit. The three parts of the human being are interlocked in a way that makes it necessary to address all if true healing is to be achieved.

The journeys toward a true awakening experienced by our patients can best be illustrated by a few examples. We once had a nurse at the clinic who, because of her interest in medicine, decided to become a doctor. While studying the long hours required to earn her degree, she started to go blind in one eye. Although aware of the importance of her sight, she persisted in her studies and, when examined by her doctors, found that she had lost 90 percent of the focal vision in her left eye.

On the advice of her ophthalmologist, she eased up a bit on her visual strain, but after a period of time still ended up with 25 percent loss in that eye. This persisted for months, until she was introduced to the Edgar Cayce readings and his suggestions for healing the body, and became convinced that she should put some of these physical healing concepts into action in her own life.

During one of the case presentations at an A.R.E. Clinic medical symposium, she felt deeply moved by the remarkable change that had come about in the healing of other patients. The nurse closed her eyes and started praying for members of her family, and at the same time asked for release from her visual problem. Although her eyes were closed, she experienced a sudden brightening of the lights in the auditorium. When she opened her eyes, her vision had returned to normal.

Subsequent examinations confirmed what she felt had happened—that her eyes were healed. Was it the wonderment and the excitement she felt about the healing in another person that sparked the same kind of response within her own body? Perhaps it was her prayers for others. Whatever changes occurred in her own physiological activity, the end result was that she could once again see normally.

Another nurse working at our clinic took part in a visualization experience at a retreat held for the staff. Relaxed by the music, and following the suggestions of the group leader, with her eyes closed, she suddenly found herself (as if she were really there) looking out the window of an ancient castle, over the green lawn that stretched out in front of her. She even smelled the cold, musty odors of the castle.

The woman came out of the reverie with a start and, for the first time in her life, realized that she had lived before, in another lifetime, even though she had always resisted the idea of reincarnation.

This was a revelation to her, but it became even more clear two weeks later that the experience was given to her for a reason. It was then that her ten-year-old daughter was killed in a bicycle accident, and she was faced with a loss that few mothers can experience without a great deal of trauma, sorrow, and sleepless nights. She found, however, that her newly gained awareness that life is truly continuous, spared her much of the grief that she would otherwise have felt deep in her heart. Her life after that was never the same, as she looked at things from a more enlightened perspective.

Another of the A.R.E. Clinic patients told us of a near-death experience (NDE) which took her into a beautiful world of calm and peace as she moved along a column of light. As she drew closer to the source of the light, she felt more and more joy—but then was stopped by a voice which said to her, "Your daughter still needs you!" She felt the pangs of separation from her daughter, and all at once found herself back in her body. She was intended to remain alive for her daughter, and now she really knew it. A remarkable awakening.

Experiences like these—the people I contacted, the activities I took part in, the dreams I had, the countries I visited, the people I worked with who were searching for healing—all were for me an awakening process, quickening me to the nature of my own being, to the nature of illness, the nature of health, and the relationships we all have with one another and with Creatives Forces, or God.

And an awakening to the power of love—as we manifest it to others—can bring for each of us a new awareness of reality, a new-found consciousness of who we really are. In the process, the steps that we choose to take to awaken to that state of awareness will become progressively more clear.

In the field of medicine, the healing of the body is a responsibility that has been traditionally placed at the doorstep of the physician. Whether this is the way it was intended to be in the beginning or not is beside the point. That's where we are at the present time. But simple healing of the physical body is not enough.

True healing is the destiny of every person on this globe, whether in this life or the next, but it must involve actual changes in the consciousness of the cells within the body, for healing is always a spiritual event.

One of the outstanding physicians of our time was Felix Marti-Ibanez. He was an eloquent and gifted writer, and his essay on "To Be a Doctor" (*MD,* vol. IV, November 1960) has become a classic in the field of medicine.

His words challenge every physician to be more than merely a scientist working mechanically with the human body. And his message is just as valid today as it was more than thirty-five years ago. "Only by knowing the healthy man can we cure him when he falls ill . . . To be a doctor, then, means much more than to dispense pills or to patch up torn flesh and shattered minds. To be a doctor is to be an intermediary between man and God.

"An ideal of service permeates all our activities; service especially to the patient, as a fellow creature isolated on the island of his suffering, whom only you can restore to the mainland of health. For that purpose you must know thoroughly not only the diseased but also the healthy . . . Learn to live perceptively, using that key to wisdom that comes from seeing everything with a total perspective and in view of eternity."

That picture, framed in the context of eternity, makes for a vision that has not yet been discovered by the medical profession as a whole.

Healing the body, then, should not be confused with the practice of modern medicine in today's world. True healing is a concept that generally has been held in disrepute. To gain a diagnosis and institute a treatment for the disease has been much more acceptable and "scientific." Healing, instead, still smacks of the superstitious or the pseudo-religious to the majority of physicians. But the real cause for an illness remains to be dealt with. It lies in the mind, the emotions, the physiology, and the endocrinology of the body and—eventually—in the spiritual nature of the individual, for we are all, in the final analysis, spiritual beings.

All through my life, in my schooling, in college and medical school, in my church and family life and my years working at my profession, I've sought, in one way or another, to explain my deepest nature. For I find that I think, I imagine, I can speak, laugh, and cry. I can create in many ways. The animals around me do not do all these things, and God made them, too.

Why do we, then, have these capacities, why these dreams of the Creative Sources? Why are we gifted to create music, paintings and sculptures, poetry, great buildings, bridges and roads, and an infinite number of things designed to make our life better and more productive? These are reasonable questions, are they not?

As you read these pages, you may find answers to some of the questions. Remember that your awakening can start at any moment, but the process requires attention to the rules and how they are to be applied. Sometimes, the rules are not easily found, but they are there to be discovered and utilized. One of the keys in designing your own awakening might be found in another of those Cayce readings—but remember that a key only opens a door. You must then find out what lies beyond the door. Let's explore the direction and discover what healing might really mean in your own life. Here's one of those keys:

For, the application in self, the try, the effort, the energy expended in the proper direction, is all that is required of thee. God giveth the increase. 601-11

The mind needs to be explored first, for it is the builder and the origin of effort. The body is the result of what the mind has created, but we don't really know the internal workings of our bodies any better than the mysteries of our minds. The spirit is the life force that allows all the rest to take place. We are eternal beings, and we need to pursue our search for healing from a perspective that accepts our soul's journey through time and space. These three parts of ourselves constitute the framework of this book, and we should find riches from the Cayce readings that will help us along the way.

Way down inside ourselves, we have never really forgotten our true nature. We are spiritual beings and will always be spiritual beings. The problem is that we do not remember consciously what it was like to be in the spiritual realm before we were born this time around. And it is only in a rare moment that we vaguely recall our past life experiences on the earth—perhaps when we meet another person in a certain situation, or awaken from a dream with a recall that tells us that we have lived before. This discovery on the part of the mind is a beginning.

Then we need to understand, too, what this body is that we live in. Why are we in a dimension that is all energy, with basic building blocks we call atoms, which apparently have no substance at all? Even though we are in reality built of these energy units, why does it seem that life is dependent upon our physiology, the functioning of our organs and our systems? This may become more apparent as we start to see ourselves as body, mind, and spirit, all three, and recognize that each has its part to play as we manifest here on a three-dimensional plane as a physical human being.

The body, however, is what we can see, feel, touch, and hear, and it demands attention. There are physical, as well as mental, emotional, and spiritual laws, and these are wonderfully inter-locked as they make themselves known as illnesses or malfunc-tions of the human body.

So we need to know more about what sort of a body our soul has created this time around, and where illnesses might actually have their origin. As we progress in this journey, you will be asked to look at how your body functions when you grant it that qual-ity we call consciousness. Does the immune system, for instance, have awareness of what to do when the body is threatened with harm? Does one of the cells of the intestinal tract know how to conduct its own affairs? Does it have consciousness?

Is the body, for instance, a conglomerate of awarenesses that make for a living human being that can be either coordinated or awash with confusion and turmoil? Is it energy in motion? Atoms with a consciousness?

We say that we are body, mind, and spirit, and we seem to be more comfortable and knowledgeable about the body and mind than we are about the spirit. However, the spiritual part of our be-ings are constantly in touch with and part of the Creative Energies that brought us into being. If we are to search for healing, we need to be more aware of our spiritual nature. That *must* be part of the healing process.

We need to come to the understanding that both illness and health are always in the process of developing. The cause of illness generally can be traced to a process that started somewhere in the past and gradually became evident at a later point in time. If you've had cancer, for instance, you probably know that it began with one cell going crazy, losing its identity, in a sense, and then replicating itself over and over again. After hundreds of genera-tions of such growth, it becomes evident as a lump in the groin or a mass in the stomach, or such. All of this, of course, takes time. You may have had cancer since one cell went awry, but at that point you didn't know it. By taking certain steps early on in the game, you might have reversed the trend, brought your immune system back into action, and healed your body from cancer without ever knowing that you had it.

Life is like that. We are always changing and influencing our body physiology for better or worse. So we are becoming ill or are overcoming illness every moment of our lives. It's like the score and the fortunes of a football team. You may be behind, but lo and behold, there is still time, and you can use the right magic and win the game. "It ain't over till it's over!" as Yogi Berra said about the game of baseball during the pennant race in 1973. And that is what the mind can do when it brings hope into the illness equation, for hope often brings about change, and change can bring about healing.

The encouraging thing about all this is that you can consciously choose what happens to your body. We all have the right answer deep inside ourselves to encourage health, but first we need to identify the answer before we can use it. That, too, is part of the mystery and part of the joy of the search for enlightenment.

I recall a patient of mine who had been diagnosed with a duodenal ulcer—one that had partially healed, then recurred, time after time. This was early in my career and I was not as aware of the mental/emotional causes of illness as I am now. He had experienced several tragedies in his life, and died at the relatively early age of fifty-eight. He was fearful of many things. His adrenal glands were overworking at a level of anger, and he rarely let anyone know about it. What he hid within his own body brought about his final illness. Perhaps there was a time when he could have let go of his anger—he could have been more forgiving, laughed a lot more—and perhaps he might have avoided dying at such an early age, by becoming more fulfilled before taking that final transfer into another dimension.

One participant in a recent Temple Beautiful program, a beautiful eighty-six-year-old woman, as we were talking about creating health through change, said gently, "Some folks find it easier to die than to make changes." And, as a matter of fact, it is often a more socially acceptable decision.

Are we then, in this day and age, waking up to the truth about what we are, and how we can do something wonderful about it? I think so. We must all start the process from wherever we are at the present, since the future is there for us to create as we choose. Our life's journey is there for us to define and participate in without illness and disease.

CHAPTER 3

Understanding Illness

Many years ago, I was walking along a path that bordered an overgrown ravine. It was sunny that day and I was really enjoying the walk. The birds were everywhere and I especially loved the repetitive songs of the mockingbird—beautiful tunes out of God's nature. One of the bluebirds settled on a bush to my right, down toward the ravine, where the side of the gorge was overgrown. Where it lit, I caught a sudden gleam of light on the ground. It was almost like the color of a rainbow, and as I moved my head a bit, it changed from a brilliant yellow to an orange—very beautiful.

I had to look at whatever it was that was sending me a signal. Carefully, I edged my way down the side of the embankment. There it was, this bright thing—a crystal, beautiful and quite large, and it looked as if it had not been touched by human hands! So it became mine, and I started back up the side of the hill.

But something made me look back, and I thought I saw another "something" that just didn't seem to belong out there in the open, near those bushes. It was golden in color and it had a beautiful rich sheen to it. This time I hurried over and picked it up. It was indeed a piece of real gold, the size of a misshapen plum. The mystery deepened.

I wondered, could there be an answer to this puzzle down in

the bottom of the ravine? The bushes obscured my view, but I needed to find out what was down there. So I picked my way through the bushes, down the steep slope of the embankment, almost falling at one point, but finally I reached the floor of the ravine. There, not ten yards away, was a broken backpack—nothing else. I looked through it—no treasure, no gold, no more crystals. I was disappointed. I thought I had something like a lost treasure, but now all I had was the problem of finding my way back to where I had started. I looked around, and decided this would not be easy. I'd have to take it one step at a time, but I could make it.

Often, our choosing to visit an unknown place, such as I did on the mountain, can be likened to the choices we make that lead us to an illness or at least to some disturbance in our innermost physiology. And to get back to where we began may also require that we go step by step.

> *Depend more upon the intuitive forces from within and not harken so much to that of outside influences, but learn to listen to that still small voice from within . . .* [239-1]

The interesting fact, however, about both the adventure I had and the adventure of illness in the body is that we participate in them without knowing what will be found at the end point.

It is not strange, then, that every human being seems to be subject to a different kind of disturbance from that of his neighbor. Inheriting a tendency or an actual genetic disease from one's parents is enough to bring a unique set of health problems to each individual. But when we become aware that our environment can affect us in a multitude of ways, then the picture of our differences becomes even more understandable. When we add our individual lifestyles and dietary habits the difference is accentuated even more. And we still have our emotional responses, our unconscious content, the astral urges, and our ability to influence the physiology with our conscious mind to add to the equation, obviously giving each of us a different relationship with our bodies and their functions.

Our life support systems bear the brunt of any adverse energies that may be coming from inside or outside, and it seems that the result is either health, a state we call dis-ease (a feeling of uneasiness), or actual disease or illness. And all of these are relative in their effect. One can begin to understand how a disease is never an entity in itself—being more of a relatively common set of symptoms that derive from the physiology of the body malfunctioning in one's own specific manner. Difficult to make a diagnosis out of that, isn't it?

Edgar Cayce gave a reading (902-1) on "the human ailment known as the common cold." Some of the excerpts are typically oriented toward the singular distinctiveness of each human being in his consciousness, but it is interesting, too, that Cayce sees the common cold as a "universal consciousness to the human body." He goes on to discuss the subject at length.

> *Thus it is almost as individual as all who may contract or even come in contact with such.*
>
> *Each body, as so oft considered, is a law unto itself. Thus what would be beneficial in one for prevention might be harmful to another; just as what might have beneficial effects upon one might prove as naught to another . . .*
>
> *First: A body is more susceptible to cold with an excess of acidity OR alkalinity, but MORE susceptible in case of excess acidity. For an alkalinizing effect is destructive to the cold germ.*
>
> *When there has been at any time an extra depletion of the vital energies of the body, it produces the tendency for an excess acidity—and it may be throughout any portion of the body.* 902-1

This reading seems to be saying that both the cause and the correction of something as simple as the common cold are almost universally individual. With the common cold, however, Cayce repeats more than once that keeping the body alkaline will go a long way toward preventing it from catching a cold.

The physician needed most is within self. The physician is the Christ Con-
sciousness . . . Do not trust in forces other than those that are within self.
Remember, thy body is the temple of the living God. [3384-1]

Some people truly are born to get sick. They cannot avoid it.
Some gain their illness almost at the time of birth, and never re-
cover. Others become ill a bit later, but never grow to maturity. We
all know this to be true. There are congenital diseases and those
of the newborn. So the valid question that follows naturally is
"*Why* was I born to get sick?"

There is a story in the Bible that bears repeating for several reasons. First, the man *was* born blind. Second, he was born this way
as a part of his life purpose, not because he had sinned in a previous life or because his parents sinned, but so that his healing
might manifest the glory of God. And third, his healing came
about instantly, and with the application of an ointment of mud
and spittle. Remarkable incident, isn't it? This is the story:

"As he went on his way, Jesus saw a man blind from his birth.
His disciples put the question, 'Rabbi, who sinned, this man or his
parents?' Jesus answered, 'He was born blind so that God's power
might be displayed in curing him. While daylight lasts we must
carry on the work of Him who sent me; night comes, when no one
can work. While I am in the world I am the light of the world.'

"With these words he spat on the ground and made a paste
with the spittle; he spread it on the man's eyes, and said to him,
'Go and wash in the pool of Siloam.' [The name means "sent."]
The man went away and washed, and when he returned he could
see."

You might want to read the rest of the story in John 9:8–41.
Jesus, in effect, told his disciples that this man was not born blind
because of the sins of his parents, nor because he had sinned in
past lives, but rather because he had agreed before he was born
that he was willing to go through life blind until he met Jesus and
could be healed. Jesus and his disciples understood, obviously,

that both of the other causes of blindness were possible, hence the question.

We all need to learn more about ourselves. And if sickness has a lesson for us to learn, whether it is how we might serve, or whether there is more about ourselves that we are being given the opportunity to find out, then we probably, at the soul level, understood that illness of some sort was destined to come about, as a means of learning how to become more one with the Divine.

So our physiology is shaped by myriad energies, showing up from the experiences of our many incarnations in the earth and the directions we have chosen to take over the ages, for one reason or another. Sometimes the energies are in the form of symbolic karmic diseases, so shaped that the lesson we refused to learn in the past is given to us in a different way that allows it to be learned through patience, persistence, and consistency, in loving our fellow man, no matter whom that may be. Sometimes it is just ourselves that we need to love. But we need always to keep it in mind that there are no conditions of the body that cannot be returned to normal. We may not currently know the means, but the reality is there.

In the experience of a disease, we often realize that it has left us in a state of depression—mild or severe—and we feel as if we are lost somewhere in the darkness of life's exigencies, and we want desperately to see the light somewhere. Deep inside ourselves, we know there is a lighted way, and darkness just obstructs our vision and we don't know where to go.

Sometimes the death of a loved one can change a person's direction in life, and if the reality of life after death is not really understood, the emotions and the feeling of anger and loss can carry on through the remainder of that person's life experience. My dad had this kind of thing happen to him. He was deeply in love with his wife, my mother. I was only seven when she failed to survive a surgical procedure aimed at helping her overcome pulmonary tuberculosis. My father was devastated. He told my two brothers and me about what happened and that our mother would not be back. We didn't fully understand, but the mark on him was much deeper.

He was angry at God for taking his love from him, and he was never really able to get over the effects of his loss. He never re-married, even though he lived another thirty years. Finally, dia-betes and a stroke were too much for him to handle. He was comatose for more than a month, then passed away in his sleep one night.

I have worked with dreams and recorded them for more than thirty-five years, so I wondered for a long time why I wasn't dreaming at all about my father. Finally, after a wait of more than a year, the dream came. I was standing outside a two-story house like those that were common in Ohio when I was born, and on the outside of the house I saw a staircase that led up to the second story.

I decided to go up the stairs, and I had reached the halfway point when a man obstructed my progress. "Where are you going?" he asked. I replied, "I am going up to see my dad." The man was kind, but firm. He smiled understandingly, but said, "You cannot go up there. Your dad is sleeping." That's where the dream ended.

No more dreams about him and no contact for a long time. But eighteen years after Dad died, I had this experience in guided im-agery: I was in a slightly altered state of consciousness after taking seriously the suggestions being given, and I found myself in an outdoor setting, very pleasant. Partway across the lawn I saw my father. He was sitting with his back to me in front of a drawing board, where he was working away very intensely. He looked to be about forty or forty-five years of age, had his hat set on the ground beside him, and was dressed in a suit, looking very well indeed.

I approached him from behind and, when I got close, said, "Hi, Dad!" He looked up as if he had maybe heard something but didn't know what it was. I repeated it—"Hi, Dad!"—and it star-tled him. He still didn't know what was happening, and he stood up, confused, looking around. Suddenly, he saw a light in the distance, and it then became the central focus of his attention. He was fascinated. He reached down, picked up his hat, and off he went, walking toward the light.

This experience reinforced something I had known for such a long time. Illness, no matter whether it is of the mind, the emotions, the physical body, or the spirit, urges us to turn toward the light. That's why we want instinctively to get well, even after what we call death, for illness is one way of understanding our separation from that which is the Light of the Universe.

Edgar Cayce often recommended light as a healing force, as well as in essence the power of life itself. The infrared or violet ray lamp, or the ultraviolet lamp, even sunshine itself, were all suggested at one time or another for therapeutic use. They were intended to bring healing in a variety of ways, sometimes killing bacteria, sometimes bringing about an absorption into the blood and tissues of substances that had been taken earlier by mouth.

Norman Vincent Peale told a story (in *Guideposts*, April 1989) about an alcoholic who had gone angrily from one church to another asking for healing of his affliction. When he ended up with Peale, he said he didn't want to hear anything about God. He was sick of hearing about God. When Peale told him that "God is in charge here!" the man stormed out. Peale wrote that as the man walked along, "denouncing the very idea of God, suddenly an unearthly radiance lit up the dark street. Buildings glowed with it. The faces of passersby shone with it. Even the sidewalks seemed bathed in it and he himself was full of light."

Fascinating, isn't it, that the alcoholic found his own body to be so changed that it was filled with light. Of course, the man never drank again, and he kept Dr. Peale informed of his welfare over the years.

Ray Moody, who set traditionalists back on their heels several years ago by recording near-death experiences (NDEs) and writing three books on the subject, described the near-death experiences frequently as including a tunnel of light and a light beyond, which is most often indescribable. He related in *The Light Beyond* (Bantam, 1988) one of the most amazing tunnel experiences he had ever heard. The tunnel was almost infinite in length and filled with light. "These beings aren't composed of ordinary light. They glow with a beautiful and intense luminescence that seems to permeate everything and fill the persons with love. In fact, one person who went through this experience said, 'I could describe this as "light" or "love" and it would mean the same thing.' Some say it's almost like being drenched by a rainstorm of light."

Light is such an intriguing phenomenon. I was in Medjugorje, Yugoslavia, several years ago with a group to visit with some of the young people who had been having visions of Mary, the mother of Jesus. Many of the thousands of visitors there had experienced unusual events. Among these, some claimed they saw Mary, some saw lights at night around the church where she regularly appeared, others reported a light phenomenon. They told us that many were able to look directly at the sun and not blink nor suffer any visual damage, attributing it to the presence of Mary at that place.

One day, I walked by the field next to the church and saw fifty or more men and women looking up at the sun. So I tried it, staring directly at the sun for three or four minutes. It appeared to me as if there were a cap directly over the sun, with light streaming out all around it. The sky was cloudless, of course, and there weren't any caps, but it reminded me of the stories of those who described their near death experience and had no pain with the light they saw, even when they approached it more closely and no matter how bright it became. It was a common occurrence, apparently. No eclipse, of course. Was it really associated with the unusual events surrounding the appearances of the Virgin Mary? Most people who were there think so.

In the Bible, light is dealt with on numerous occasions. "God is light and in Him is no darkness at all" (John 1:1–5). In John 1:8, Jesus was called "The true light, which lighteth every man that cometh into the world." In Matthew 17:2, "His face shone as the sun and His raiment was white as the light."

In the Old Testament of the Bible, it's interesting to look at the plague of darkness which Moses called down on the Egyptians (Exodus 10:22–23): "And Moses stretched forth his hand toward heaven; and there was a thick darkness in all the land of Egypt three days . . . they saw not one another, neither rose any from his place for three days; but all the children of Israel had light in their dwellings." And from Psalms 36–39, "For with Thee is the fountain of life; in thy light shall we see light."

Paul, you may remember, was on the road to Damascus, when "suddenly there shone from heaven a great light round about me." He was blinded by this, receiving his sight back later—all for a great purpose (Acts 22–26).

But let's not forget that we, as creations of the Divine, are also beings of light, as yet mostly undiscovered. As such, we can be healed in a variety of ways, because light is indeed life.

When such information is first presented to the body, it may realize and declare "Why offer spiritual counsel, when I am so anxious about my physical being as well as those about me?" But who healeth thy diseases? To whom does the material world belong? Man or God? Whom do ye serve— thine own appetite, thine own desires, or God? These should be thy first approach. 3538-1

CHAPTER 4

Holistic Medicine in Action

When we are searching for a definition of what healing really means, we need to know what healing is and what it is not. The field of medicine is not a healing profession. Chiropractic, osteopathy, naturopathy, physical therapy, acupuncture—as they exist today, these are not healing professions in themselves (although some practitioners do qualify as healers). They all exemplify approaches toward correction of an illness, and as such, do a good job when used creatively. However, by themselves, they do not bring about healing.

Healing can only be accomplished when the individual human being—the mind of the one in need—is activated (either from within or without) to allow a divine change to come about within his own body; and when the body is treated in such a manner that physiological abnormalities are influenced so that they might return back toward a normal balance.

A change in consciousness must happen, a new direction in light must be taken—in other words, a divine change must occur within the consciousness of the cells and atoms of the body itself. For the mind and the spirit (the source of life) are found not only in the brain, but in every system, organ, cell, and atom of the human body.

Edgar Cayce had this to say in talking about the nature of healing as he saw it from an altered state of consciousness.

All healing, then, is from life! Life is God! It is the adjusting of the forces that are manifested in the individual body.

Then, there must be periods of reaction of the bodily forces, the bodily functionings, the bodily response to influences without and within; and then the necessary attuning again and again. [2153-6]

To heal in that manner can really be called holistic healing. We must look at our fellow human being as having been created by God; in His image; as having a mind that is the builder; and as having a body that is the result of the mind being active and creative, using the spirit as the force of creation itself. This is the story that has been available in the Edgar Cayce material since he started giving readings early this century, nearly nine decades ago.

The term "holistic," as it is applied in the field of medicine, had its inception in the late 1960s. Dr. James Windsor gave a lecture on mental illness at the second annual medical symposium sponsored by the A.R.E. Clinic in Phoenix, Arizona, entitled "A Holistic Approach to the Care of the Mentally Ill." And the term "holistic medicine" was born.

It flowered over the years, leading to the formation in 1978 of the American Holistic Medical Association, and then to an editorial in the *JAMA (Journal of the American Medical Association)* on March 16, 1979, which reads that "The roots of present-day holism probably go back one hundred years to the birth of Edgar Cayce in Hopkinsville, KY. By the time he died in 1945, Cayce was well recognized as a mystic who entered sleep trances and dictated a philosophy of life and healing called 'readings.'"

Dr. Windsor would not argue with the *JAMA* statement, for his paper used the Cayce readings as the primary source of his data.

Why would Cayce be pointed out as the originator of the idea of holistic medicine? Because of his psychic information, of course, that repeatedly stated that each human being was body, mind, and spirit. Even in the readings he gave for those who were ill, he repeatedly indicated that illness could be the result of disorder of the body, in disobeying the laws of the human body, or it could be the mind, where the mind has been used in a destructive manner in this or other incarnations. Or it could be a defect in the understanding of the spiritual origin or destiny of the human soul, and actions taken in line with those mistaken understandings.

In talking about illnesses, Cayce saw the individual as an eternal spiritual being, a soul, coming into the earth plane time and time again to experience events, activities, and illnesses here as a series of repeated steps to bring about soul growth.

In discussing how healing comes about, he generalized often about methods of healing but became specific in what really needed to be done in order to experience true (holistic) healing:

> While true, medicines, compounds, mechanical appliances, radiation, all have their place and are of the creative forces, yet the personality of arousing hope, of creating confidence, of bringing the awareness of faith into the consciousness of an individual is very necessary.
>
> For who healeth all thy diseases? Only when any portion of the anatomical structure of a human being is put in accord with the divine influences, which is a portion of the consciousness of an individual entity, may real healing come. Without it, it is nil and becomes more destructive than constructive. 5083-2

> Yet, when one is in any environ, one is subject to the laws of same; and unless material laws are spiritualized in the mental activity of souls, those oft that are healed physically remain sick spiritually. 559-7

> Healing of the physical without the change in the mental and spiritual aspects brings little real help to the individuals in the end. 4016-1

Cayce was consistent in indicating that a spiritual growth was a necessity for healing.

The structure of the body is designed by Divine intent and action to allow the human being to perform whatever physical ac-

BLONDIES BARN LLC
5640 MARSH
HASLETT, MI 48840

TERMINAL ID: 008604522
MERCHANT #:   376204811990

MC
M×××××××××××2661
SVR: 5
SALE
BATCH: 001370   INVOICE: 070054
DATE: DEC 28, 10   TIME: 14:20
SQ: 022   AUTH NO: 735025

PRE-TIP AMT $10.05

TIP   _____

TOTAL   _____

        CUSTOMER COPY

tivities need to be done to fulfill one's purpose for this incarnation, and to move the soul in the right direction—toward its source.

Further, Cayce pointed to the organs and systems of the body as life-supporting, life-giving functions permitting us to continue activity in this dimension.

And the senses were created so that we might be aware that we really are souls journeying in the earth, awakened to our environment and conscious that all events can be learning experiences to use as stepping-stones on our way upward. And he always warned against us using them as stumbling blocks.

My experience has taught me that these concepts of holism are as real as life itself. Mankind—all of us here on the earth—are made in God's image and are eternal beings, and need desperately to be recognized as such when being cared for in the field of healing, no matter what discipline we are working with. It's difficult to recognize our eternal nature, for it is not a common concept in our culture and our Western religions. However, its most dramatic effect is to let us understand that we have been here since before the world even came into being, and will be in existence after the world has ceased to be.

Illness is so closely associated with one's goals and destiny that they cannot be separated. The disturbances of the body are to be treated as opportunities to look at ourselves as what we are—eternal beings. With our negative emotions, we alter the nature of our endocrine organs, which in turn disturb the function of our intricate physiology, through our nervous system and hormonal activity. Given enough aberrant physiological activity, the disease we are creating comes into sight, eventually being diagnosed when it becomes strong enough to manifest the appropriate symptoms. It is only then, in most instances, that we take steps to normalize the body, through whatever steps we take.

Much needs to be developed in understanding about how this body of ours works its way through this incarnation, but we can begin by acknowledging that our lives really are a manifestation of consciousness. What does it mean in terms of consciousness and holistic healing to have hit bottom, and to have decided that we do *not* like it?

One concept that I have found useful in helping me to look upward when I've hit bottom is to decide to be content where I am, but not satisfied. Why be content? If I am a malcontent individual at that moment (and our moods can change every few moments), then my inner parts will be disturbed—to a degree they will be in turmoil. That only spells need for a change in direction—it doesn't help the healing process. I know I deserve to be there, so I need to be content, to be willing to assess the situation and move gently and lovingly with my body, but be aware that I am not satisfied to stay where I am. Since this is the fact, then I take a different direction from what I have taken in the past. I change course.

In a sense, it's like taking a tour of Europe or the Middle East. We choose where we plan to go, but when we get to the third destination on the agenda of our trip, perhaps we experience gunfire close by which seems dangerous. We do not want to get involved in a war, we want to continue our tour. So we quietly talk to the tour director, letting him know that, of our own free will, we chose this course, but now we want to make another choice and head back home. We change direction.

But to be content in consciousness means that I need to be aware of what I am and what my possibilities are—at least in the field of being healed. I believe I am eternal and I am created in God's image. I've got potential that I've never even dreamed of, as do we all. Cayce had much to say about potential.

All knowledge,—then, now, or in the future,—is latent within self—would man but begin to understand. The stamp, the image of the Creator is a part of the heritage of each soul. Thus all knowledge that has been is a part of the experience of the soul. The entity here,—seeing, experiencing the unfoldment in all varied groups, as in homes, taking their place as individuals and no longer as herds or groups controlled by others, but as free men,—sought that knowledge in self, by its experience of unfoldment and the aiding in the forming of plans, as they unfolded, with the others who encouraged the entity in that period of activity. A-1, 2533-4

Cayce, of course, was giving counsel to an individual who was asking for help in his own life. But the story is the same for every individual on the face of the earth. We all have that "stamp of the Creator" as a part of the heritage that was given each of us in the very beginning. We can claim it and begin acting as if we have it at any moment in our experience of living in the earth.

We have the opportunity to be content where we are when we realize that we have that divine potential, for we know that eventually we will be in touch with it and will be living it. Perhaps not now, but perhaps in the time frame that Jesus talked about in the Bible, when he said, "In your patience possess ye your souls!" (Luke 21:19). At the same time, we are not satisfied to remain in our present consciousness, but choose to move to another, higher level of awareness.

Sometimes, divine potential shows up when it is not recognized and when the holder of the potential does not even know it exists. And it often occurs in the healing process, which for everyone is part of the adventure in consciousness. A good example of this is a patient I'll call Fred, who showed up at the A.R.E. Clinic with a three-month history of swelling and redness in his right foot and ankle, and recent development of back pain. He had been tested for rheumatoid arthritis and the latest test returned positive. Fred was sixty-five. Aside from these problems, he had been in excellent health.

His regimen of therapy followed very closely the suggestions given in the Cayce readings and in the circulating file on arthritis: Atomidine in a cyclic series, Epsom salts baths each week, full-body massage (at the clinic) followed by local peanut oil massages on his foot and ankle each night before retiring, visualization techniques, and a diet especially for sufferers of arthritis.

His response was rapid. In two months the swelling was gone, there was no discomfort or stiffness, and for all intents and purposes, he was well. Follow-up exams gave us reassurance of the permanence of Fred's quick recovery.

Rheumatoid arthritis does not respond in such a manner in

medical literature except in rare, undefined cases. Yet Fred did re-
cover quickly. Perhaps the "stamp of the Creator" was more active
in him than we might recognize from the outside. He may have
just thought, There is no big deal about this. If I do these things,
I'll get well! And he did. We, too, can tap into holistic healing on
many levels, including even the search for longevity.

Much has been written regarding the aging process, which
must be reversed or stopped—or at least slowed down—if one is
to enjoy that quality we call longevity. With 140 years of life a real
possibility in the years and decades to come, we first need to
know what it is that causes an aging process if we are to slow it
down. We usually think of longevity of the body in terms of
health, muscular vigor, family history, and related genetic inheritance. However, we rarely include what we *think* about longevity
as a factor.

Cayce outlined our potential for longevity by telling us that we
have all knowledge at our disposal, down deep in the nature of
how we are created. And this would include, naturally, the knowledge of how to live to any age.

Perhaps it is the thought forms we create that tend to make the
body what it is. This is the position taken by the Cayce readings,
and those thought forms will always be found in the unconscious
mind. If we create belief patterns that say we do have unlimited
potential, then we have tuned in to the infinite and have that
knowledge at our disposal. The next step is to call upon that
knowledge in faith, for faith is one of those keys.

Cayce talked about longevity in a way that is not generally
found in our medical training. He simply said that if we gain the
consciousness the body can replenish itself from within, we don't
need to undergo aging. However, our departure from this dimension comes about for most of us when we succumb to the pres-
sures that arise in the normal affairs of the day, or to the unusual
events that come in to everyone's life. To keep the kind of compo-
sure that will allow one to ride out all the vents of the world with

equanimity is quite a job. Yet that is the suggestion given, to use if we choose.

A decision to leave the body through death most likely comes about when we don't focus in on our association with the Divine to a great enough extent to draw on the power that is there. When that happens to us, we simply get tired, and say, "That's enough for this time." And that's really understandable. Suppose, for example, one partner passes through the door we call death, and the spouse who is left behind misses the other deeply or perhaps has not really had the opportunity to say good-bye and subsequently feels overwhelmed and saddened by daily existence, enough to want to stop living. Sometimes we refer to this as dying from a broken heart. Often the body and spirit are too tired to continue on alone.

The other side of the coin, however, is that when one does focus on his true divine power, amazing things can happen. This would explain the many instances of individuals living a long time. Their offering in this incarnation serves as an example to their fellow man of the possibilities of longevity.

If you choose to dig deeply into your resources, know that the consciousness of every cell in your body will be there with you. Metaphysically speaking, you will never be the same again. Holistically, you will have begun a process necessary for total body healing. As Cayce remarked:

> *Thinking adds not one whit to thy stature materially, but mentally, spiritually, it may produce the revolution which brings peace and harmony into the world.* 3384-3

But what happens when disease is present, in relation to holistic healing and longevity? What we call a disease covers a host of bodily conditions, but it is reasonable to say that all have a beginning in a point of time, and all will eventually come to an end, like everything else in this earth plane of existence. The beginning may never come to our attention at the time, for it may be as simple as having an argument with a spouse. It may, on the other hand, be quite significant, like an angry divorce situation, where a spouse says "This relationship is killing me" without realizing the literal implication of that statement.

Whenever there is stress in that manner to the immune system, the injury to that portion of the body is not easily repaired, for the emotion may not be healed but remains as a scar deep in the unconscious mind and in the emotional centers. This scarring could be the beginning of illness that will affect the heart, the nervous system, the cardiovascular system or really any other part of the body. For all systems are subject to being injured, as long as the hurt continues.

Let's suppose the heart is the target organ, along with all the blood vessels, arterial and venuous. If this were your heart, wouldn't you want to treat it properly to prevent heart disease? It would be best, of course, to start as soon as possible, before you need a cardiovascular specialist. To begin, look at how your emotions have fared over the last six to twelve months. Have you taken any measures to counteract the stress of daily living?

These measures are not new, having been reported by the sleeping Cayce in a variety of instances, and in a thorough manner. Recent scientific studies show that Cayce's suggestion for healthier lifestyles have done more to reduce the risk of heart disease than medical treatment, including a more healthful diet: fewer or no cigarettes; lots of green vegetables, fruits, and whole grain foods; fish, fowl, and lamb for protein; as well as the avoidance of fried foods, white flour, and white sugar. Of course, we would add to this list constructive attitudes, positive emotional patterns, enlightened belief patterns, exercise, and the daily use of meditation and prayer.

It is easy to postulate that the major message to the average American is that you can do more to lower your own risk of dying from heart disease than your doctor can do for you. Actually, you have remarkable control over your own physical destiny. This idea is repeated over and over in the Cayce material. And it helps bring to our awareness that our emotional stresses have been part of our adventure in consciousness since even before we were aware we might be in the process of becoming ill. We even knew that we have always been involved in such an adventure.

Once the disease, as an entity, has come to our attention, then we are definitely interested in bringing about a resolution of this that seems at times to be threatening our very existence. That brings about a more serious attempt to correct the way the body is functioning, or in some way stop the disease.

To resolve this condition that threatens us always involves the quality of time and the strength of the mind. Disease may be cured in a moment, as when one sincerely prays and the illness is gone, for example. One of our patients had been taking medicine for a heart condition that had been diagnosed as angina pectoris. He was resting on a relaxing device that delivered a very weak electromagnetic field to his body. He was half-asleep when he suddenly "saw" Mary, the Mother of Jesus, in front of his mind's eye. It was as if she were *really* there, and he knew that instant that he was healed of his heart trouble. He told us all about the experience, of course. That was fourteen or fifteen years ago, and he has never had any further heart trouble, nor has he needed medicine for his heart.

Resolution to a disease can happen instantaneously, and the usual methods of explaining it fail to make sense. But it has happened and it can happen, and it is the part of many individuals' adventure.

On the other hand, the overcoming of an illness may take days, weeks, months, or even years. Healing can come as one enters God's other door, or it may even be put off to be met in another incarnation, if our stubbornness in learning a lesson is too strong.

Cayce was asked once about the time factor in healing. His answer, as it usually does, talks about the question, but adds depth to the answer.

Can healing be instantaneous or is it always progressive?
A-15. The natural bent is progressive, but this does not indicate it may not be instantaneous. For, as the operator progresses in the experience, to be

every whit whole in any way, either in self or the one being treated, it is to be immediately healed. But, as has been always—and ever shall be, the progress, or the maintaining of that attained is through growth. For, to be healed immediately and then be separated and gradually lose self—how has it been given as of old? He that looketh, and he that has gained the concept of the spirit of the influences in the infinity and turns back—the last estate of that man is worse than the first! 443-6

Healing, in the context of the Cayce material, is certainly an adventure in consciousness; and healing the whole person then becomes a responsible action for both the doctor and the patient involved. As man moves into a new age of consciousness, this concept needs to be part of the consciousness of all people.

We need to recall again that behind every experience of illness lies a prize—a pearl of great price, a life lesson that helps us in our adventure to be headed in the direction of the light. It can be found, but it needs to have the seeker active in searching.

The bodies that cause disturbance by the disobeying of the laws and activities in a material world are but troublesome things to the soul at times. LIFE IS CONTINUOUS! The Soul moves on, gaining by each experience that necessary for its comprehending of its kinship and relationship to Divine. 1004-2

CHAPTER 5

The Mind in Control

The mind exists in all parts of the body, not just the brain. A portion of our mind, called the autonomic nervous system, is always active, even while asleep, controlling the unconscious activities of our internal bodily functions, giving us the gift of life. The cells of the body even have memory, another function of the mind, which often teaches us when we are young not to touch something that is hot. Our fingers give us that message.

Techniques, such as biofeedback, can let our conscious mind enter the domain of the unconscious and teach our bodies to lower the body temperature or lower the blood pressure—really a host of other mental abilities. The mind can dispel a migraine headache, place ourselves in a sleep condition, even into an altered state of consciousness.

Our mind uses the power of choice to determine what we are going to do today. We take on a task that our mind believes we can do, and it most often is accomplished.

In 1969, a group of fellow travelers and I, under the guidance of Hugh Lynn Cayce, asked the Dalai Lama how his people were able to walk on fire and not be injured. He told us that they made themselves one with the fire.

"For example, if you take the heat of fire, generally speaking, it

could burn you and you can feel the heat. But if you are to analyze it and come down to the atoms that create this fire, if you are
able to take the atoms apart and if you utilize this knowledge, it
will not have the power to burn you." He went on, "When fire
burns us, it is because we have not been able to analyze either the
fire or the real nature of our own bodies. When you are able to understand the physical body and external objects, the combination
will enable you to perform miracles." Our group was still unable
to understand the method by which we could be "one with the
fire."

Less than a week after that, we visited some fire walkers in the
Fiji Islands and had a practical lesson in how to do it. Seven native islanders—all men—walked repeatedly across stones that had
been nursed to a white-hot heat by fire that had been built in the
fifteen-foot pit and kept going for several days before the event.

Their native grass skirts were singed, sometimes burned, but
I personally examined a fifty-five-year-old man and a fifteen-
year-old boy after they had finished their fire walking. The soles
of their feet were totally unharmed, a bit dusty from the earth
and probably from the bits of ashes they may have picked up,
but no pain, no burns, and they seemed to have a good time and
a lot of fun exhibiting their abilities to a large group of Ameri-
cans.

Did they make themselves one with the fire? They didn't mention it when they talked to us. They said they were part of a group
of families who were able to do this. Born into these families, the
males could learn to walk on fire. Even if a man were to be mar-
ried into one of these families, he could do the same thing—*if* he
believed he could. It seemed that these Fiji Islanders instinctively
knew the power of belief, a function that seems to be of the mind,
but has its roots in the spirit and its manifestation in the body.

There are many remarkably unique qualities about these sometimes frail bodies that we inhabit, which have inherent powers of
healing as well as the power to create illnesses and dysfunctions
of the body. And the mind has control in building all these facul-

ties. We are really in control of our bodies if we utilize the mind appropriately.

From the New Testament, you might read the story of Jesus raising Lazarus from the dead (John 11:43), and of Philip being transported bodily and instantly to Azotus (Ashdod) on the Mediterranean from a place described as "the way down from Jerusalem unto Gaza" (Acts 8:39–40).

The Bible is replete with stories that substantiate a different law taking effect at times: Jesus disappearing from the midst of a hostile crowd trying to kill him in Nazareth (Luke 4:29–30); Elijah placing his body over the dead child and bringing him back to life (1 Kings 17:21–24); and Jesus making the blind to see (Matt. 9:27).

One of his disciples (Matt. 15:30) reported that "Jesus now returned to the Sea of Galilee, and climbed a hill and sat there. And a vast crowd brought him their lame, blind, maimed, and those who couldn't speak, and many others, and laid them before Jesus; and he healed them all."

Jesus walked on water, stilled the elements of the weather. He healed people by word, by touch, and by simply being there. There are countless stories about healing, considered by true believers to be miraculous. How do we come to an understanding about events like these?

Padre Pio, a devout parish priest and healer in Italy, was probably best known for levitating at times while giving mass. Those who followed his teachings and loved him dearly cared for him more because he was able to pray for them and they were healed. This was commonplace. He was also able to bi-locate. While he was sitting in meditation, people would see him at the same time at their bedside, blessing them, or simply walking in the street.

For fifty years, he carried the stigmata that mirrored the wounds Jesus incurred at His crucifixion. On September 23, 1968, at the age of eighty-one, and on the fiftieth anniversary of the beginning of this phenomenon of stigmata, Padre Pio died.

Theresa Newman lived for many years in Bavaria, taking only

one wafer at mass each morning—no other food. She was closely scrutinized by physicians, but always they found her to be eating nothing else. She would work out in the fields, and would also on Friday go through the experiences, in an altered state, that Jesus suffered at his crucifixion. Paramahansa Yogananda visited her once and told her that she was born to demonstrate that man does not live by bread alone.

Yogananda himself (*Autobiography of a Yogi*), when he entered *mahasamadhi* (a yogi's final conscious exit from his body), was not embalmed, but lay, unchanged for twenty days, until the Forest Lawn Mortuary placed the bronze cover of his casket in position. The director sent a letter to the Self-Realization Fellowship which reads, in part, "The absence of any visual signs of decay in the dead body of Paramahansa Yogananda offers the most extraordinary case in our experience . . . No odor of decay emanated from his body at any time. . . . The physical appearance of Yogananda on March 27, was the same as it had been on March 7, the night of his death."

On another trip that I took with psychic researchers, I saw a movie of a Russian woman, Nelya Kulagina, levitating a Ping-Pong ball in the air, using only energy from her hands. Later on, when we had lunch with Nelya, without touching a wedding ring that was placed on the dinner table in front of her at the Leningrad Hotel, she used energies that she said came from her hands to cause the ring to move across the table and drop off on the other side. How can we explain such phenomena?

The unusual nature of the human being has been an enigma throughout the history of man in the earth, and this is only a very small sampling of amazing events that have been seen and reported from a variety of sources. How are all these things possible, even granting that some of the stories through the years might have been exaggerated?

Obviously, the body is truly not what it seems to be to the casual observer. If we understand that our bodies are the means by which we—as spiritual beings, as souls—are able to play a part in this dimension, then we can unravel a bit more of the mystery. For the soul, made in the image of God, has capabilities far beyond our imagination, for the most part untapped, and essentially unlimited. There is consciousness and creativity in each cell, even each atom, of the physical body and the mind is the builder, the controlling force, always. Cayce explained it this way to one person:

> *For each cell in the atomic force of the body is as a world of its own, and each one—each cell—being in perfect unison, may build to that necessary to reconstruct the forces of the body in all its needs . . .* [93-1]

We are not solid, as we discussed earlier, but instead are composed of atoms and molecules, under the control of electrical or electronic impulses, mediated by our brains and nervous systems, but truly generated by our eternal soul bodies. Most anything is possible, given that we find out how to do it. The "how" is usually the problem.

There are those, however, who have learned some of the lessons needed. And we all have the destiny within our own beings to develop whatever is to be beneficial to our own pathway through life and that which may also aid our fellow man. Since our purpose in the earth is to learn how to be more like God, then it is the divine plan or set of rules that we need to understand and follow.

> *Know that in whatever state ye find thyself, THAT—at the moment—is best for thee.* [369-16]

In spite of the biblical injunction that we are made in God's image, and therefore spiritual in nature and eternal beings—that our real life, origin, and destiny are in another sphere—we still pinch ourselves and wonder how our real life can be somewhere else and not here. On earth, we can see, hear, feel, taste, and smell our environment. It is "real" around us. If an ironing board drops on our foot, it hurts. When a bullet passes through your heart, you die. We are born as little beings, and we grow in size and stature until we are adults. How can we be real in other than this material plane of existence? Aren't we solid flesh and bone?

We are really energy in motion, atoms flying around in a miniature world, creating molecules and more and more complex structures until we are organs, systems, and moving parts.

Atoms are not solid. If certain atoms are split there is an explosion. Atoms are constantly being split apart in the sun, creating light and heat, fire and energy, all of which makes possible the environment that we live in here in the earth.

It's safe to say we are a mystery, at least to our conscious mind. And the earth, too, may be a mystery which we have not begun to understand. From the Cayce standpoint, the earth is a manifestation of the Divine, set in space for us to enjoy, and to use in order that we may grow toward the Divine.

So it appears reasonable that, if an atom is nonmaterial, we—as formed beings—are not really material either. But we *seem* to be solid, we *seem* to be material, although what seems to be may not necessarily be the reality. Nevertheless, this manifested realm is not the same as the dimension from which we have journeyed to be here on earth. That unrecognized dimension has a different reality. It is the *real* life, the real home, the place where we recognize our eternal nature, and the place where we had our origin and will experience our destiny.

> For with God nothing is impossible, and the individual that may give himself as a channel through which the influences of good may come to others may indeed be guided or shown the way. [165-24]

Our search and eternal struggle to return to our place of origin is the cause of our anxiety, for somewhere, deep in our minds, we know instinctively that this earth is not our true home.

It is also safe to say that the mind of man in the world today cannot comprehend the essence of what God really is. And since we are made in this image, we need to create some sort of symbol that describes God, and then, one that describes man. For man was made in the image of God, yet certainly is not God. Let's look at it as I've shown in Diagram 1.

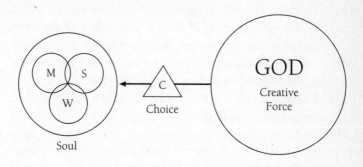

DIAGRAM 1. CREATED IN THE IMAGE OF GOD.

The Creative Energies—God—is shown here as a circle. A circle has no beginning and no ending. Thus, for our purposes, the circle is eternal. It is well chosen to symbolize that which is God, the eternal, never-ending being.

Let's say the symbol on the left shows the soul, as created in the image of God, also having eternal life. But for purposes of acknowledging how man is thus constituted, the soul is shown as having three circles within itself, representing spirit (S), as the giver of life itself; mind (M), as that power that always becomes the builder; and will (W), the power to choose. Perhaps there is nothing more precious and valuable as our ability to choose. Everything that we have, everything that we are, gives constant evidence of the use of that power of choice, exercised through the creative ability of the mind.

As we will see later on, the mind becomes the controller of all that we do, all that we are. For we are formed by the choices that the mind takes. Our habits, our tendencies, our chosen activities, all emanate from the mind as it fashions our existence here on the earth.

Our goals this lifetime, the purposes for which we came into the earth, all come about through the power of the mind, and we must always remember that we are a soul on a visit to the earth, having received the gift of life itself through what we call the Spirit, or the manifestation of God. Our minds will direct our course and make us what we are to become, while we remember that we are at the present moment the result of what we have built with our minds in this and even in prior lifetimes.

Looking at yourself for a moment, you might reflect on what Edgar Cayce had to say in these two selections:

> *Your personality, then, is the material expression. And your individuality is the personality of the soul* [2995-1]

> *Their individuality and their personality don't reflect the same shadow in the mirror of life.* [3351-1]

From what Cayce was telling these people, it seems that your soul manifests your individuality in the spiritual dimension (the place we go to when we die, or where we were before we were born), while your personality is what you are expressing or being while you are here in the earth life. And it is interesting that Cayce suggests that these two qualities of you cast or reflect different "shadows in the mirror of life."

In other words, we may discard much of what we think we are when we die and exit our bodies.

Our real self, however, remains what we were in the beginning, with much added through experiences that we meet in this life and have met in other lives. The essence and content of life remains, and is carried into each successive life. Thus, I remain *me* throughout my existence, throughout all my lifetimes, and the periods in between. I am eternal, so it remains that I cannot quit. There's no place to go! I am here this moment, which, we come to understand, is all the time we ever have. We don't have yesterday, for it is gone. We cannot grasp tomorrow, for it keeps fading away in the mist of life yet not lived.

We can choose to live this moment in a way that will bring us closer to that goal we sought out before we were born. The goal, the purpose: to know ourselves to be ourselves, yet one with God or the Creative Forces.

What, then, is WILL? That which makes for the dividing line between the finite and the infinite, the divine and the wholly human, the carnal and the spiritual.[262-81]

In order to understand more about what healing is all about, we need to explore more extensively our nature as living beings. We continually need to challenge our accepted concepts and be ready to open ourselves to our potential, as truly made in the image of God. If God created the universes, and created us in His image, what does that say about our potential? It's difficult to comprehend, but try to imagine what it may be saying.

Jesus was challenged by the Pharisees when he said, "My father and I are one!" They were going to stone him because of his blasphemy, where he, a mere man, claimed to be a god. Jesus answered, "Is it not written in your own Law, 'I said: You are gods'?" (John 10:31-35). In the Old Testament (Psalms 82:6) the Psalmist added "and all of you are children of the most high."

Jesus took it further when he said "He who has faith in me will do what I am doing, and he will do greater things still, because I am going to the Father" (John 14:12, 13).

We need to stretch our imaginations at this point. Scientists, trying to understand how the worlds came into being, using the "Big Bang" theory, suggest that the solar system, and the universe itself, is perhaps more than 5 or 6 billion years old.

Cayce told stories about our origin, our beginning, in a dimension beyond time. However, if we are to put it into time concepts, which seem to rule this world, we are told that you and I were in existence even before the worlds came into being. That makes you and me over 5 billion years old! Not only that, but we keep on going—and growing!

Where does this concept come from? Cayce said in his readings—and in his waking life, too—that one would benefit from reading the fourteenth through seventeenth chapters of the Book of John, and "know that it speaks to Thee." Then Cayce always added his own perspective from Universal Sources, which amplifies and stretches us even further about our nature. Here he is, quoting Jesus:

> "He that takes my yoke upon him and learns of me, with HIM will I abide day by day, and all things will be brought to remembrance that I have given thee since the foundations of the world, for thou wert with me in the beginning and thou may abide with me in that day when the earth will be rolled as the scroll; for the heavens and the earth will pass away, but my word shall NOT pass away." The promises in Him are sure—the way ye know! [262-28]

In John 17:5, Jesus was praying, "And now, O Father, glorify thou me in thine own presence with the glory which I had with thee before the world was made." There Jesus was referring to his own presence in that time when the worlds had not even been formed.

Cayce reminds us of this state of being more than once. Again, as he commented on the material in the Book of John, he had this to say:

> The activities should come to be less and less for self, but more and more than self may be the channel through which the Glory of the Father may be manifested in the earth.
>
> Then, the activities of self become less and less towards the Glory of self, less that good may come to thee. For being one with the Father, even as He has given, "As ye abide in me and I in the Father," then there may be that Glory, that consciousness of the oneness that thou didst occupy before thy advent or before the world was. Even as He prayed, "Now, glorify thy son, that he may have the glory that was his before the worlds were." [262-93]

This staggers the imagination, especially if we are to give credence to what Jesus had to say, and if Cayce truly tapped the Universal Sources. In my perception of how things are put together, and in my own experiences in this world, there is little doubt that our existence is eternal, stretching both into the past and far, far into the future.

> *For the Will may be made one WITH HIM, or for self alone. With the Will, then, does man destine in the activities of a material experience how he shall make for the relationships with Truth.* 262-81

CHAPTER 6

The Conscious and Unconscious Mind

As you read these pages, you are certainly using your conscious mind, storing information away, or perhaps rejecting it. However, while you are active in this regard, your unconscious mind is busy at a host of other tasks. Your unconscious, you see, is the storehouse for not only the control panels directing all the life-support functions, but also the memories of all that has happened to you in this life, and in those lives that have faded far into the past.

The unconscious likewise plays host to habits of response regarding dietary likes and dislikes, activities that have become habitual, plus all those emotional reactions that have been created in the past but seem to come from nowhere, most often when least expected.

And the unconscious is always active through its physical counterpart, the autonomic nervous system, in keeping the body's life-support systems going.

Part of the whole picture might become more understandable, if we look at Diagram 2, although neither pictures nor words can simplify the magnificence of the human body.

To understand this form from a perspective of consciousness, then, let's look at the diagram, remembering that the C enclosed by a triangle will always represent the word "choice" in these charts or graphs.

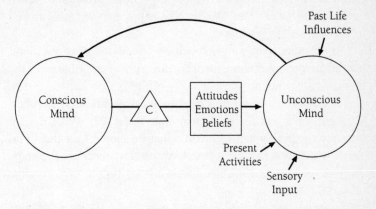

DIAGRAM 2. THIS IS THE ACTIVITY OF THE CONSCIOUS MIND WITH THE POWER OF CHOICE, USED TO CREATE HABITS IN THE UNCONSCIOUS MIND, WHICH THEN IS ALWAYS GIVING FEEDBACK TO THE CONSCIOUS MIND.

We must remember that the conscious mind *acts*, while the unconscious mind *reacts*! In Diagram 2, our present activities—the use of our physical body in many ways—are constantly being logged into our unconscious mind to create reflexes, habits, and instinctive responses. Too, the direction given that part of the mind from the senses contributes to its content and the responses. It needs also to be remembered that all those past life experiences and influences make themselves at home in the unconscious mind.

However, the choice, as it is applied to attitudes, emotions, and belief patterns, always directs *how* we tread our chosen path, but not necessarily *what* work or service we accomplish. That is a separate kind of a choice, dependent on many factors—the family we are born to, the kind of life work we have had in past lives, experiences in this life, and so on. So we can serve others in our jobs as teachers, nurses, physicians, secretaries, or travel agents, for instance, with a smile or a frown. Our face to the public may be a conscious choice at the moment or the result of what attitude has been consistently taken in the past and stored in the unconscious mind as a normal response to most any kind of situation in which we might find ourselves. We can be a happy person inside as well as to others if we practice.

To do more than simply touch on the mysteries of the mind would be presumptuous, for who can truly know what is in the mind—conscious or unconscious—of the person sitting next to us? Let alone the mind of a mathematical genius such as Albert Einstein, or a humble but remarkable Padre Pio. What does it mean in the Bible when we are told that we should have that mind in us which was in Christ Jesus? We need to allow for the enormity of the potential of the mind, while starting to explore some of these abilities.

So we need to look at Diagram 2 once again. We have used this power of choice over the ages in fashioning what we are today. In the act of creation, we were first souls, given life, through what we call the spirit. The soul also was given a mind and the ability to choose. When we came into the earth plane, we needed a body in which to experience the reality of the earth and its environment. Creation of that body, then, gave us the full set of capabilities we needed to live fully on the earth.

Then, through the power of choice (which we will explore more fully in the next chapter) we fine-tuned the body, much as any sports star would strive to do, so that he might excel. We can fine-tune the mind associated with the fingers so as to type, or to write creatively, to become a Beethoven or Mozart, or we can strive toward the same kind of goals that Einstein achieved. We even have the ability to develop our spiritual senses so that we are more perfectly attuned to the Creative Forces of the Universe—the sort of thing that Jesus manifested. Much, indeed, can be done in instructing the unconscious mind of our bodies so that we can become more than we are at the moment.

Our memories are stored in the unconscious—memories to be recalled later of what went on today, and in all the todays of the past. The past life memories can be drawn from the storehouse of such memories, generally called the Akasha or Akashic Records. When Cayce gave a life reading, he ascended up a column of light and arrived at a great hall where a white-haired old man led him to a book, which contained the story of a man's past lives. Some have likened this storehouse to a great tapestry which each individual weaves as he lives in the earth plane.

We have in our unconscious minds the habits, the genetic patterns, the autonomic controls that support life itself, that allow us to do all the myriad activities that we perform every moment we are awake. So we might say that everything our body has sensed and experienced is placed in our memory tank because of the choices we have taken in the past and are taking at the present moment.

It should never be forgotten that there is a key for us to use in developing into the sort of spiritual being that was our destiny when we were first created. The power of choice gives us the ability to use that key. Application of our choices in the material world is the key. We can choose to be godlike in our emotions and feelings, our attitudes and beliefs, and in our interactions with others. Or we can choose the opposite, and lose ground in our quest.

Only when there is the full application of self in any phase or activity in which the Creative influences or the ideals are manifested, does there come peace.

When there is the application rather for self-indulgence, self-aggrandizement, or only for material gains, then it eventually brings distortion, disturbance, and distress—even into the material and the mental and the spiritual aspects of an entity. [1862-1]

The recorded contents of an unconscious mind do not, necessarily, then, give us guidance toward the ultimate goal that was ours from the very beginning. That part of the mind simply helps to make us what we are today. The guidance comes after learning what the path is toward our destiny, and then choosing the emotions that make the path richer, the attitudes that clarify our mental directions, and the belief patterns that tell us, deep in our hearts, that this is the way to go. That is the critical step shown in Diagram 2, and it produces in the process new patterns, new habits of emotions and attitudes and beliefs that will then lead us without the same kind of effort that was ours previously.

Very complex, isn't it? Yet, Jesus pointed out the complexity in a moment of clear universal truth: "This is my commandment to you: Love one another" (John 15:17). Simple, isn't it?

Perhaps we can get the complexity of the picture aligned with the simplicity of the action, and find that we may come out of it with a body that is healthier and a relationship with God that speaks volumes to the very heart of each of us.

The conscious mind needs always to be available for the body to use in this dimension and thus improve the world for being here. So let's look at the diagram again as it explores the relationship between the conscious and the unconscious minds.

The conscious mind is always choosing, and it formulates the attitudes and emotional patterns which it then places in the unconscious mind. It always chooses its beliefs—which tells us that it is quite important to know what our ideal is, so we can choose appropriately. But the placement of those qualities into the unconscious mind has to be repetitive, or they simply do not find their way into the unconscious as thought forms or patterns or habits, call it what you may.

Persistence, patience, and consistency are paramount in creating the desired reactions from the unconscious. And in the diagram, there is always feedback from the unconscious mind that leads us, in moments of unawareness, to believe that we are *just born that way*. We even say "that's just the way I am" without realizing that "the way we are" is an amalgam of those habits we repetitively manufacture in the unconscious mind. Good, healthy mind habits, then, can yield positive results, as evidenced in this anecdote:

It was a usual day at the A.R.E. Clinic until the woman who

had come in for a complete physical exam told me about her experience with a tumor of the breast. Her story provided me with an example of how strongly a belief can be brought into the unconscious mind—so strongly that it can heal the physical body.

She had felt a lump six months ago and had at once consulted her doctor, who sent her to an oncologist. A mammogram was performed and a suspicious mass was uncovered. The doctors felt it should be biopsied for cancer.

She went back home and said to herself—this cannot be! She knew about the Cayce work with castor oil packs, so she fashioned a pack that would fit on her breast and wore it every night for four months. She went back finally to the doctors who had taken the earlier mammogram, and had the test repeated. The mass was gone! Of course she was proud of her accomplishment and joyfully told me the story. It was a major life event—she believed that the castor oil pack would get rid of that lump in her breast, and it did.

I've often thought that the body and its mysteries are like space and its vastness, like the atom and its minuteness, for we understand none of these with our present, finite minds—even as we understand God only partially and our own spiritual nature with dimness of vision. But it is our challenge to charge ahead and try to gain more knowledge as we go about our daily tasks in life.

The nature and content of the unconscious mind is a mystery in that it is beyond our conscious awareness—thus *un*conscious. But our self-created attitudes in that unknown part of ourselves often thwart our attempt to be healed.

Such a thing happened to a fifty-year-old man I hadn't seen for more than five years. He looked a bit older, and as if he had been through many rugged life experiences. He gradually unfolded his story, which was more eventful and stressful than any similar period in his entire life. Arthritis disabled him and following the experience of the Temple Beautiful program and a five-year therapy plan, instead of being less of a problem, it was obviously a bit worse. His lack of improvement challenged me, so I began questioning his habits.

His castor oil packs were only occasionally used. He took his Atomidine for two weeks and then forgot to take it, except sporadically. He could not take the Epsom salts hot baths because it was difficult for him to get into his small bathtub. His massages were sporadic, and the violet ray treatments he was supposed to be getting were virtually nonexistent. Besides, he worried constantly because of the problems he still had resulting from his divorce some six years prior to his first visit to the clinic.

He sheepishly admitted that he had not been consistent with his therapy, he was not persistent, and certainly was not patient with his body and the way it responded. It reminded me of one of Edgar Cayce's remarks about these qualities:

> Do as we have given, and we will bring the near normal conditions for this body. Be persistent, but be CONSISTENT with the applications— also, don't expect the results in one treatment! For it's been many seasons coming on! 5503-1

Part of the very nature of love is consistency, persistence, and patience. In this earth dimension, where time is a factor, we have the opportunity to experience all of these as a living experiment, and this in turn makes of these activities a habit pattern in our lives and moves us closer to our destiny, a true eternal oneness with the Creative Forces of the Universe.

So, unwillingness to be consistent, patient, and persistent was the real problem for the man with arthritis—especially when he knew what he needed to do. It's breaking an age-old law, knowing what to do and not doing it. It always backfires on us and we pay the price.

Yet, when we fail to accomplish a program of therapy that has promise of at least a partial healing of the body, there is a promise that comes from the Cayce readings that gives a ray of sunshine when it seems so dark. When one keeps trying to bring healing to the body, but fails in his efforts, there is the reassurance that God sees the try as righteousness. The only time one truly fails is when he stops trying. Sometimes, it is very important for us to recall to mind that healing is always a spiritual adventure, a journey toward an eventual endpoint that we only vaguely perceive in our minds. This probably could not be better said than in the advice given to a woman who was faced with the diagnosis of scleroderma:

> *Do these, as we have indicated . . . Not as rote, but knowing that within self must be found that which may be awakened to the building of that necessary for the body, mentally and physically and spiritually, to carry its part in this experience. For the application of any influence must have that which is of the divine awakening of the activative forces in every atom, every cell of a living body.* [726-1]

So, how is it that we are healed? What is the magic formula? Do we need to look at our past life experiences to gain insight into the cause? Is that a requirement? Perhaps the answer is much more simple than we would think. Possibly the acknowledgment of what we really are is the very first step. We were created in the image of God. God is love, and as we manifest love in our relationships with others when we meet day by day, we are one with love, thus one with God. And healing comes.

> *You find yourself a body, a mind, a soul; each with its attributes, manifesting in a material world. And you realize that the body, the mind and the soul are one—and that confusion may cause detrimental influences to body, to mind or to soul.*
>
> *Then, you must have your ideal as to spiritual values, as to spiritual imports in your experience. And know, whatever may be your desire, it must have its inception in SPIRITUAL attitudes.* [2030-1]

CHAPTER 7

The Power of Choice

There is no question in my mind that we could live to be 140 years old if we were to follow the rules of health that are readily available to us today. But it requires choosing to adopt a health-producing lifestyle rather than continuing to overeat, underexercise, and abuse the body with alcohol, drugs, and living patterns that are destructive emotionally, spiritually, and physically.

How much does the body suffer when one holds inside himself resentments toward a spouse, a supervisor, a parent, or an authority figure? How many days does one lose from his life expectancy after carrying those resentments inside his being for a year or two or maybe even five years? Who knows the answers to such a question? Yet we keep those feelings deep inside our unconscious minds all the time, and tell others that "it doesn't bother me."

Nevertheless, the body moves closer to breakdown whenever the tension or the resentment, the anger, finds itself a home in the unconscious. Subsequently, of course, these feelings appear as abnormalities in the functioning physiology and in the tissues of the body itself.

Perhaps we choose to allow these death-hastening events to

come about because we deny that it has even happened; or we can't find anyone to help us; or we don't want to be perceived as inadequate and unable to deal with stress. Of course, there are many other excuses, but we tend to hold these hurts and frustrations inside ourselves and cause eventual death-dealing blows to our body.

Our choices often spell out the length of time we will spend in this incarnation. Moses challenged his people before he left them with these words: "Today I offer you the choice of life and good, or death and evil" (Deuteronomy 30:15). Then he urged them to choose life, that both "you and your descendents will live." History recounts whether the people followed Moses' instructions, but they *were* given the choice.

And today, we, too, are given that opportunity to exercise our choices. We can smoke or not smoke. We can exercise or not exercise. We can do drugs or take prescription drugs or not take them. We can harbor grudges or let them go. We can forgive others or condemn them. We can love or hate. And this list could go on at length. We could even follow the instructions that Moses gave his people or refuse to do so. For, in a very real sense, we are his people.

God gave us the capacity to choose. He gave us the gift of free will. This is the nature of the soul. And it goes with us every instant of our lives, is always there to be exercised or to be left unused. Cayce explained God's gift to man in one instance as follows:

> He made the individual entities or souls in the beginning . . . Having given free will, then—though having the foreknowledge, though being omnipotent and omnipresent—it is only when the soul that is a portion of God chooses that God knows the end thereof. 5749-14

It is rather interesting that from the perspective outlined in the Cayce readings, even God cannot keep us from choosing, and doesn't know what we are going to do before we choose our path.

This speaks highly of the power He has invested in us, for we can indeed do what we choose to do. We can follow the path that God has outlined for us, to create harmony and light and love, or we can allow the darker forces lodged in our unconscious mind to take over, and create confusion, anger, vengeance, and destruction.

It seems to me also that we can exercise our willpower to bring about constructive influences in other people's lives or the opposite—a destructive reaction. We indeed have power that we seldom realize is ours, to manifest change in our own bodies and minds or in the world around us.

Let's look again at how this might work. In Diagram 2, we see that the conscious mind throughout all our previous lifetimes certainly had the same setup in choosing the attitudes, emotions, and beliefs that are shown in the diagram as existing today.

So we built into the unconscious mind certain habits of reaction by acting out in those lifetimes the choices that seemed appropriate, or by choosing to adopt patterns of emotions, attitudes, or beliefs given to us by parents or others who may have said, "This is the way we do things in this family," or this country, or this church, or school, or political party, or whatever. We gave up our right to choose in those instances, of course, probably because we did not know that we could have chosen to do differently.

This lifetime, however, we have been awakened. We have set out on an adventure in consciousness that tells us we have a power now, that was hiding from us, that allows us to change, to create, to build, to create new standards, and to set out on the path that leads us back to our roots—not in the earth, but in the heavens, where God created us in the beginning and is waiting for us to make our way back home.

Then, given that our unconscious storehouse of past creativity is not exactly what we want, how do we go about changing it? It's a bit like a computer, isn't it? The unconscious has been programmed; the information secured there is much like a world of habits, for we react emotionally—by instinct, it seems—much as we react physically when a ball is suddenly thrown toward us. We try to catch the ball, unless we have never taught our body how to do such a thing in the past. If we have learned that little trick, however, we respond or react quite well.

The emotional response when someone challenges our reality is to take what has been formed in the past and react with anger, or fear, or maybe even with humor or with interest. It all depends on what has been ingrained in our consciousness. We are ready always to respond habitually, automatically, without our being consciously aware of our response.

So how do we go about changing these habits that appear like magic and disturb us because they do not measure up to what we would like to be?

Cayce's suggestion was very simple. He said that everyone could use this method: "We correct habits by forming others" (475-1). The key, of course, is our power of choice. We *choose* to create that which is more in line with our ideal, with the goal we wish to attain, and gradually let the other habit pattern go.

Look again at Diagram 2. The conscious mind is active every waking moment and is using the power of choice whenever it chooses to do so. From the moment we choose to love another human being instead of hating him—a major change in consciousness—to the next very material moment when we choose to avoid a piece of chocolate candy instead of eating it, we are going about the business of changing our lives.

It is important to remember, however, that one choice does not create a habit. The choice has to be made over and over again, until the new habit is stronger than the old one. And the choice has to be completed with action by the body. This is how progress is made, and it strengthens our understanding of the need to be persistent, patient, and consistent in the effort to heal the body—a suggestion Cayce emphasized over and over again.

> That man has been endowed with free-will, free-choice, is his birthright. Do not cast it aside, nor sell it for the gratifying of any material thing in thy experience that is merely passing. But the CHOICE must be within thine OWN self. The ways may be set before thee—the CHOICES must be TAKEN of thine own consciousness . . . Being aware of what ye would that the Lord would do with thee, what THOU would do with the opportunities, the privileges He hath bestowed upon thee as one of His children. [1470-2]

Memories from the past are not all stored away in the brain. One of my patients, a fifty-six-year-old woman, told me she was certain that in a past life in France, she was sent to the guillotine. She told me she was too stubborn to learn the lesson that brought her to her death, but was reincarnated once again, rather quickly. This time she was beheaded again—by the executioner's ax.

In her present life, she was born with a red mark around her neck. Apparently her memory exists not only in her brain, but in the tissues of the neck. There was undoubtedly strong emotion associated with both of those lifetimes in France, and even more with the manner in which she died.

I had the opportunity to interview a man in India some years ago who told us that he remembered his last lifetime as a captain in the German army in World War I. He hated the killing and the misery of what he was doing and vowed that when this was over, he would go somewhere where there was no war. He didn't make it in that lifetime, for he was killed when a bullet struck him in the neck and severed his spinal cord.

He was then reborn in India, a place where they indeed, at that time, did not have wars. But his eyes and his hair did not reflect an East Indian genetic pattern; instead, he retained his blond and blue-eyed genes, amid all the other kids in the Indian village, who had black hair and brown eyes.

He managed to avoid a great deal of peer pressure in school by dying his hair black, and eventually he became a CPA. When I talked to him, he had been working for the Indian government a number of years. He told us that he traveled in his work to various countries and was invariably greeted with the question, "Oh, you're from Germany?" And he disciplined his children like a traditional German father.

I asked to examine the area where the bullet had supposedly hit him during the war. On the right side of his neck I found a depressed scar—the kind one would expect from a deep wound that had healed. It had been there since his birth, of course, a remnant of a fascinating memory of trauma and deep emotions, carried over from a past life.

These examples illustrate that cells of the body have memory beyond the ability to remember what their specific job is in the functioning of the body. They also have the kind of memory that impacts their being by emotions of anger, frustration, or joy, to mention just a few, as well as the hurt that comes from physical injury. The German officer carried over such strong feelings of longing for peace, a desire that had been shattered by a death-dealing bullet, that his body remembered.

The body—the spiritual body—is like that. But, we wonder, where does this ability to remember reside in the body? Where do we look to understand how this kind of thing can happen?

Sometimes, we say we have "buttons" that others push. Our reactions are predictable, usually destructive, most often in anger or defense. Or we say we have "old tapes" that we replay. Again, the response is predictable.

A friend of mine who has worked with the Cayce material most of his life had a remarkable dream which led him and those of us who heard it to a new level of consciousness. He dreamed that he went swimming in deep water. He found a vertical tunnel which went on down deeper. He was almost bursting in need of oxygen when suddenly there were lights and colors and bubbles and movements surrounding him, and he found that he could now breathe without needing air.

He ended up in a kind of auditorium where, with his wife, he was attending a meeting. A man in black cape and headgear stood in front of a podium, and there were rows of people sitting on chairs. The man at the podium told the people, "All those interested in black magic hold up your hands." Our hero and his wife at first wanted to be part of the group, but then said, "No, we will not take part in any black magic!"

Then they saw Memorex cassette tapes beside them which were records of different parts of their lives and past lives, and they knew that the black magic could only be used through these tapes. My friend woke up at this point.

In discussing the dream, the message became obvious. Our destructive negative actions (the black magic) can come about only when we allow others to push the buttons that turn on the recorder and then "play the old tapes." Health certainly improves as the state of the unconscious mind improves, and this can happen in many ways. But we need to toss away the old tapes, one by one, as we move along.

While we understand that memory of traumatic events may reside in the tissues of the body that are affected by the trauma, we need to look elsewhere for the full memory of past lives and their experiences to determine where emotional and attitudinal memory reside. In the Edgar Cayce readings, we are told most frequently that these memories reside in the endocrine glands, or their counterpart, the seven spiritual centers. This may be because emotions and feelings, which are part of every human experience, find their origin there. And they stay locked up in those compartments until they show up either in our reactions or in our dreams.

> *Each soul . . . should come to this realization: It is not in the earth, or manifested in the earth at this time, by chance, for God is not mocked—and whatsoever a soul soweth that must it also reap.* [5343-1]

CHAPTER 8

Your Seven Spiritual Centers

Cayce often pointed to the endocrine glands—seven of them specifically—to teach a fascinating lesson in the integrity of the consciousness of the human body by relating those seven glands to the mystical spiritual centers that are known in the Eastern religions as chakras. And they are indeed provocative and exciting.

The endocrine glands are both physical and spiritual. Each has a mind of its own, which directs the hormonal output into the bloodstream and the neurological impulses into the nervous system. Each of these endocrine glands also has an energy component.

Psychics who see energies in the body that are not seen by others have described a vortex arising out of each of these seven glands much as I've shown in Diagram 3. Some researchers think this is energy originating in the body, while others feel it is actually energy drawn into the body through these sensitive areas.

The seven glandular centers might be shown as small circles within a larger circle. In this way, relationships could be symbolized and better understood. We could imagine the seven centers as seven members of a family, five children with the mother and father.

Now, if there were only the two parents to consider, there would be just two relationships. To carry this analogy a bit further,

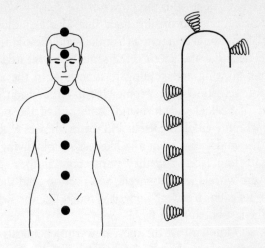

DIAGRAM 3. VORTICES ASSOCIATED WITH THE SEVEN CENTERS.

however, we can see that when the parents have a child, the number of relationships magnifies. Each member of the family suddenly has two other people to deal with. This totals six relationships, quite a change from the two that were there when they started.

How about the family of seven members? Each of the seven has to deal with six different relationships. Now we have forty-two total relationships in the family.

To go back to the seven glands: Since the spiritual/glandular centers have consciousness, and since each of these seven is related to the other six through the nervous system and the hormones in the blood, and probably also in consciousness, it becomes obvious that each human being has a group of amazing consciousnesses inside his being—every one of them different because of past history and experience. The emotions, the attitudes, the responses, the feelings—all are different for each center, work differently in any given situation. It is these seven areas of consciousness that make each of us humans unique, the product of what we have done with the power of the spirit flowing through our bodies. It's not surprising, then, that we are all different.

I've often thought, in trying to understand these emotional patterns better, that the seven centers might be regarded as living creatures, moving and shifting relationships in the air as their color and activity changes, somewhat like the vision in the first chapter of Ezekiel. A whirlwind came out of the north like a cloud, with fire enfolding itself, and the brightness was great, and out of the midst of it came the likeness of four living creatures, each with four faces, and they went about as they willed. And there were wheels within wheels. You need to read the entire vision. In its extensive symbology, it is much like the Revelation of John, the last book in the Bible.

It is also known that the most powerful chemicals created in the body come from these endocrine glands. Likewise, it has been found that each is a neurohormonal transducer—able to convert electrical energy into hormonal energy, and vice versa. A neurohormone is a hormone that affects nervous system function or a hormone released due to nerve stimuli.

What this means in ordinary language is that a gland such as the adrenal is a functional link between the hormones it releases and the nerve impulses it creates—or receives. Very powerful and very important.

The idea of receiving nerve impulses and releasing hormones as a result might be a key to understanding how energies that we do not yet understand could influence the very emotions that we experience by changing the energy into hormones. In other words, we may be affected by other people, their activities, and their reactions in ways that we usually do not even consider—when our hormones become energized.

The endocrine glands identified by the Cayce readings as also being spiritual centers in the human body are the pituitary, pineal, thyroid, thymus, adrenals, Leydig cells, and gonads. Endocrinology is a specialty in the field of medicine, and there are multiple textbooks and journals dealing with the subject. I will not attempt an exhaustive commentary on it. However, a simplified overall view of the relationship between the emotions, the glands, the nervous system, and chemicals affecting the body, and the symbology associated with the centers, as compatriots of the glands, is important. One cannot move very far into the study of the mind, body, and spirit connection without an understanding of some of the metaphysical aspects of our very physical glands.

The pituitary is considered the master gland and is attached to the base of the brain by what is called the infundibular stalk, a downward extension of the floor of the third ventrical of the brain. The pineal is also located under the brain, slightly higher geographically than the pituitary. It is interesting that a certain kind of lizard develops the pineal into an external third eye that appears in the middle of the forehead. Metaphysically, the pineal is considered to be man's third eye.

The thyroid is located in the neck, and the four other glands/ centers are found below the level of the shoulders. The thyroid is understood to be the site of the power to choose. The thymus is found in the mediastinum of the chest, in front of and above the heart. It is known as the director of the immune system, and called the heart center in the Cayce readings. The adrenal glands are paired and located one atop each of the kidneys. They are called the fight/flight glands because of their activity when the body is faced with any sort of an emergency or challenge, and constitute one of the major influences in the activity of the sympathetic nervous system.

The so-called Leydig cells is an accumulation of Leydig cells in the male and hilar cells in the female. The hilar cells are found in the ovaries, while the Leydig cells are interstitial cells located in the tissue of the testes surrounding the sperm-bearing cells, and are responsible for secreting testosterone into the bloodstream. The hilar cells in the female are considered to be the counterpart of the cells of Leydig.

And the seventh of the glandular centers is the gonads—the paired testicles in the male and the ovaries in the female. They are

THE SEVEN CENTERS

	Glands	Beasts	Elements	Senses	Lord's Prayer	23rd Psalm	7 Dwarfs	Colors	
7	Pituitary				Father	Cup	Doc	Indigo	H E A V E N S
6	Pineal				Name	Anoint with Oil	Sleepy	Purple	
5	Thyroid			Hearing	Will	Table	Happy	Blue	
4	Thymus	Eagle	Air	Feeling	Evil (Live)	Evil	Sneezy	Green	
3	Adrenal	Lion	Fire	Vision	Debts	Righteousness	Grumpy	Yellow	E A R T H
2	Leydig Cells	Androgynous Man	Water	Taste	Temptation	Waters	Bashful	Orange	
1	Ovaries Testicles	Bull (Calf)	Earth	Smell	Bread	Pastures	Dopey	Red	

TABLE 1. THE SEVEN CENTERS AND SOME OF THEIR RELATIONSHIPS.

very important in that they make it possible to continue the species of man in the earth. The gonads, then, are power centers.

Thus we consider the gonads to be the first in the ascending order of the spiritual centers, the Leydig cells second, adrenals next, then the thymus, the thyroid, the pineal, and the master gland, the pituitary. Each of these centers has a symbolic meaning that is reflected in many ways. Some of these can be seen in Table 1.

These chakras, as some would call them, are divided into four that are "lower" and three so-called "higher" centers. The lower ones are the material or earthly centers, represented by the bull, the androgynous man, the lion, and the eagle. They are also the four elements: earth, water, fire, and air. The three upper centers are considered to be spiritual centers, not directly related to the earth.

You can see how such divergent concepts as the Lord's Prayer and the Seven Dwarfs might be related symbolically in the chart, each having a counterpart in the seven centers.

The Cayce readings point to these glandular areas as repositories of past life memories. All interpersonal relationships bring into focus emotions of one sort or another, and these are treasured and kept in the very tissues of our glands.

It has been said that a symbol is a visible sign of something invisible. A lion, for instance, is the symbol of courage. Or it could be the symbol from dream content that indicates power or anger. In psychology, a symbol is an act or object which represents a repressed desire or emotion of which the individual is unconscious.

Past-life memories that reside in these glands are emotionally charged and repressed, else they would have been dealt with at the time the experiences took place. When they come to the surface, as in dreams or meditation or in a counseling session, they usually appear as symbols that give us a clue as to what sort of emotion has been disturbed, and where trouble in the physical body may have its inception. The bull, for instance, is considerably different from the eagle, so emotions emanating from the first

center would provide a different picture of the internal functioning of the individual than those coming from the fourth center.

The symbols, then, are understood as the language of the unconscious—how all parts of our unconscious mind communicate
with us on the conscious level. They may give us indications of
prior incarnations as well as the memory of experiences we have
dealt with in earlier times. In addition, there is much in the part
of the mind we call unconscious that is of the divine, kept from
us because we have not yet grown into that level of understanding. Yet this divine knowledge can teach us the wonders of our
spiritual heritage if we continue to ask and seek. One way to
touch the Divine is through the practice of meditation.

The meditation experience is the raising of energy from the first
to the seventh center. When one meditates, the relationship of the
human to the Divine is enhanced, the body and mind are attuned
to the spiritual reality, and a step is taken toward the oneness that
has been promised to us for thousands of years. As one meditates,
and the energy is raised up to the pineal, there is sometimes the
experience of light, such as that which Paul experienced in the
Bible on the road to Damascus; the light described by nearly all
those who have had a near death experience; the light that vi-
sionaries over the ages have reported in times of high illumina-
tion. In this experience of raising the energy of meditation up to
the level of the pineal, the energy being raised meets the energy
entering from above, creating light at this point, called by many
the point of the "Mystical Marriage." In other words, the human
meets the Divine.

*Let the body-mind continue in the attitude of seeking for the SPIRITUAL
awakening. Know that each experience in this material plane is, if used in
a constructive manner, FOR SOUL DEVELOPMENT! For He (God) hath
not willed that any soul should perish.* A-1, 1445-1

*Let each individual know that it is as a harp upon which the breath of God
would play.* 281-60

Keep thine feet on the earth, but thine head, thine soul, thine mind, to the whisperings of God! [440-14]

As we come to understand the essence and the symbology of the seven centers, we can begin to comprehend what sort of result misuse of these emotions can and does create in our bodies. At times, they set up the beginning stages of an illness that might be experienced and diagnosed at some point in the future. In the same manner, we can see how strong emotional patterns formed deep within one or more past lifetimes can create the pattern of an illness we are currently experiencing.

Often, I'm sure, we would like to ask (even if we don't), "Why am I having such severe trouble with my hearing?" Or again, "Why does a nice guy like me, doing such a good job in trying to love my fellow man, have an incapacitating illness like rheumatoid arthritis?" Or maybe, "When I've been following such an excellent diet, how can it be that I've got this severe skin rash?" The questions could go on and on, and have, as a matter of fact, been a part of nearly everyone's consciousness when the body is not doing what the individual wants it to do.

If you study the chart in Table 1, you can identify the nature of the emotions according to the kind of symbols associated with the gland. For instance, Dopey—of the Seven Dwarfs—is associated with the first center, thought to be the location where all energy in our body arises, whether it is sent upward in meditation, or used in the act of sexual intercourse. What emotion in the human family is used more foolishly than sex? Sort of like Dopey, isn't it?

The symbols used in that chart give us an indication of what the unconscious mind is trying to tell us through the physical counterparts of the seven glands. The unconscious is much more knowledgeable than the conscious mind in many regards. If we dig deeply into these areas, as the Seven Dwarfs did while searching for gold in the earth, then we must expect something valuable to be brought to light.

Our conscious mind, however, often will reject truths, claiming that they don't make common sense and are not logical. So the symbols become the costumes that cloak the truth in mystery and thus bypass the barrier between the conscious and the unconscious, bringing the truth to conscious awareness—where the symbol or symbols are then understood. It's much like the parables Jesus told His disciples. Difficult to understand through ordinary means, they become words of life only if we get the *idea*, the nonverbal message.

Those messages about our emotions and attitudes seem to be transmitted in a variety of ways, in colors or beasts, elements or dwarfs, psalms or prayers, churches or seals.

So how is it that we can understand, then, that a good friend seems to be led or driven by adrenal influences, some good, but some not so good? Perhaps the friend is often a very strong, dominating individual. He has excellent eyesight. Sometimes he roars like a lion, has a fiery temper, and wants everything done exactly *right*. When he is not pushing people around, and is relatively quiet, you might describe him as grumpy.

What does that analysis tell us, then, and what kind of trouble could be brewing or already manifested in his body? We know that the cells in the adrenal glands are not totally pure and ascended in nature. Many of the emotions are directed toward self, or our friend would not need to be dominant or angry or have a fiery temper. The glands, then, create abnormal impulses in the nervous system. Some are destructive. At the same time, hormones that are to an extent in turmoil are being released into the bloodstream and have their effect on every cell in the body.

The areas most at risk are in that part of the body where the adrenal glands are found, the mid portion of the abdomen. The liver might be weakened from the constant barrage and the body be developing liver or gall bladder difficulty. Most commonly, blood pressure would be elevated, and impending trouble in the intestinal tract would be in the making, an ulcer perhaps. The list of difficulties directly associated with adrenal malfunction is large, and varies individually depending on many other aspects of personality and glandular makeup.

Suppose that individual is the one you see in the mirror? It is not simple to be a detective in this area, especially when you are the focal point of the investigation, but it gets ultimately to the truth. Because, as we know, we still are able to choose what kind of emotions we wish to nourish and develop. That's the key to that part of the search.

The bashful person, for instance, may try to cover up his bashfulness, but if he is an observant individual, he can identify its reality, either by looking within himself or trying to understand others. All the signs point toward the second glandular center. This is the area where bashfulness originates. Here sexual differentiation is created—male or female, testosterone or estrogen, Leydig cells or hilar cells. Water, which flows in the area of least resistance, and is so very, very strong and life-giving, is also terribly destructive. Water becomes very important in that person's life. The nature of this center is marked by the sense of taste, often overdeveloped, and so important in forming habits that cannot be easily broken, such as chocolates, fats, rich foods, and even drugs.

It seems that the second glandular area is where choices must be made in directing energy from the gonads upward—it may be used for self-gratification in the act of sexual intercourse or for the experience of a deeper expression of love for another person.

It should be recognized at this point that full understanding is not likely to be achieved of the nature, use, and effect of either positive or negative impulses or hormones flowing from these seven centers. We have been in the earth time after time, and have not yet acknowledged even those few who both understood and lived the qualities of balance throughout these centers. Our feelings and thus our responses are difficult both to identify and to utilize at will.

When these centers gain a relative state of balance, and even when they are in disarray, they constantly give input to the physical body through the distribution of their hormones through the bloodstream, and their relationship to the various parts of the nervous system. Yet it can be seen that they have a very close relationship with the unconscious mind. And it must be noted that they are created and can be changed through the power of choice; while they may also be maintained as a constant habitual response. This is the usual way we see them manifested in our relationships with others. It can easily be seen that the manner in which we live our lives—the emotional outbursts or the balanced responses we may create—has a central influence in fashioning our personalities and the kind of life we will be experiencing the rest of our days here.

> *The Mind is the Builder in material things. It is that association or that connection between the material and the spiritual forces, or the without and the within, and their coordination within the physical functionings of the body itself brings that the individual builds within self.*
>
> *Then, think CONSTRUCTIVELY! Do not make for negative forces that create barriers or hardships in any way or manner. For these must eventually come back to self.* [1192-6]

The Cayce material paints the picture of emotions as residing in the glands—not as thoughts that arise in the brain, but rather as a part of the cells that make up the glands themselves. Thus, an approaching tornado, for instance, is brought to the nervous system via the optic nerves, and then almost instantaneously communicated to the mind and consciousness of the adrenal glands. They, in turn, alert the entire body to the presence of danger through the fight/flight response. Thus we see that some of the primary emotions that bring about survival share space with those that make a human relationship more precious and those that bring about irritation, frustration, and anger into our experiences.

About the time Cayce was giving his readings, emotion was defined in *Webster's Collegiate Dictionary* (5th Edition) as any one of the states designated as fear, anger, disgust, grief, joy, surprise, yearning, and so on. There are undoubtedly dozens of emotional states that could be included in this list.

Medicine gets a bit more specific and psychological. In *Taber's Medical Reference*, there are two definitions that are helpful for us to understand. "1. Passions or sensibilities characterized by physical changes in the body such as alteration in heart rate and respiratory activity, vasomotor reactions, and changes in muscle tone.

"2. A mental state or feeling such as fear, hate, love, anger, grief, or joy arising as a subjective rather than as a conscious mental effort. These constitute the drive that brings about the emotional or mental adjustment necessary to satisfy instinctive needs. Physiological changes invariably accompany alteration in the emotions but such change may not be apparent to either the person experiencing the emotion or an observer."

In Diagram 2, the conscious mind was shown as having the capability to choose an emotion, an attitude, or a belief. The beliefs are rather well understood, but it is sometimes difficult to separate an attitude from an emotion. Webster helps out on this: An attitude is a posture; a position assumed or studied to serve a purpose; or a position or bearing as indicating action, feeling, or mood; as keeping a firm attitude; the feeling or mood itself; as, a kindly attitude.

An attitude could be described as behavior toward a person, group, thing, or situation representative of conscious or unconscious mental views developed through cumulative experience.

I've thought of attitude sometimes as the direction taken. For example, if I were trying to experience the Light, I would take an attitude that would lead me toward the Light. This would mean that I would choose to live the fruits of the spirit, and that would be my attitude in my activities. These same fruits of the spirit, however, are emotions, so with that attitude, I would be attempting to change my emotional patterns, and my attitudes and emotions would be in essence the same thing. The change, of course, would only come about slowly, with repetitive actions taken that would make for more and more dominant patterns in that part of the unconscious mind or glands.

However, if I were to take an attitude of committing myself to exercise every day, this would be establishing a new pattern in my unconscious mind that works for my benefit, but does not necessarily involve my glandular structure, content, or activity. Yet it is highly important.

In the introduction to the three A.R.E. Library Series books on attitudes and emotions, Dr. Herb Puryear writes about attitudes in an especially clear manner: "An attitude is literally a stance, a posture, an orientation. It is a point of view which we chose for the moment; therefore, our attitudes reflect more than any other quality the *nowness* of our being. They are related directly to our consciousnesses; they reflect what we choose to hold in consciousness with respect to all that we confront. An attitude, because it relates to the mind and will, as well as to the spirit, is one of the clearest, most immediate indicators that man is a soul, a spiritual being."

If these emotions, and perhaps even our attitudes, are locked up in our seven spiritual centers, which are eternal parts of ourselves (as well as in those same physical glandular centers), then we are dealing with powerful and creative capabilities. In order to gain a better perspective of what we are working with, we might simply see them as repositories of memories of our past emotional relations to situations and people. When we meet the same or similar individuals in the present, we have a real opportunity to grow spiritually.

We can allow ourselves simply to react with the patterns, the emotions, the feelings that were built into the glands in those earlier experiences. For those patterns are indeed to be found right there in the memory of our glands, as habits. So we can replay the habits, no matter how disturbing they might be. It's easy to do, for it is simply a reaction. But there is always a price to pay.

Or, instead, we might choose to act differently, perhaps in a more constructive manner, with feelings and emotions that build loving relationships. We can create new habits over a period of time, which will bring an entirely different response to the same situation we reacted to destructively in a time long past.

Repeated use, then, of any chosen emotion or attitude through the conscious efforts of our minds will bring about a change in how we view the world and how we deal with it. Constructive or destructive—that's the power we have in our ability to choose.

> *KNOW THYSELF! And then ye may know the greater relationships that each emotion brings in thine experience.*
>
> *When anger doth beset thee hast thou stopped and considered what the fruit of rash words would bring? Hast thou not rather said, "Yes, I forgive but I cannot forget. Yes, I will not remember but don't remind me of what you did."*
>
> *How hath it been given? If ye would be forgiven, ye must forgive. If ye would know love, ye must be lovely. If ye would have LIFE, GIVE it! What is Life? GOD—in action with thy fellow man!* 793-2

PART TWO

The Body

CHAPTER 9

Harnessing Energy

In medical school we were never taught that all parts of the body are living units of life itself with a consciousness and a mind of their own. Physiology was defined as the science of the functions of the living organism, its components, and the chemical and physical processes involved. Physiology, we were told, was to be understood in terms of scientifically measured tests or biochemistry but rarely, if ever, in terms of consciousness, cooperation, and coordination, which bring all parts of the functioning organism into action and life in this world.

My perspective on understanding the body is based on the concept that we are all spiritual beings, wearing a body, in a sense, that is constructed of living atoms and molecules, and experiencing this dimension for special purposes which were chosen before we were born.

Physiology needs to be understood as an ever-changing process (involving our mind, emotions, and consciousness) which can keep our bodies—our atoms, cells, organs, and systems—alive and healthy. This process is always influenced by a multitude of factors that may be either positive or negative in their effect on the process.

With our power to choose, we are agents for transformation.

We are constantly, eternally, changing, for better or worse. We are always creating our health or lack of it, and the only time we have to create anything is this single moment in time as I've shown in Diagram 4. This always gives us the opportunity to take a new direction, turning toward the light, or away from it.

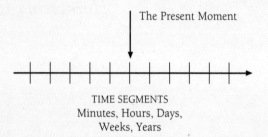

The Present Moment

TIME SEGMENTS
Minutes, Hours, Days,
Weeks, Years

DIAGRAM 4. HOW WE MOVE THROUGH TIME OR HOW TIME MOVES THROUGH US.

Time is a reality, always moving into the future, passing us by. Or, we might say, *we* are always moving through time into the future, taking those moments that are passing and depositing them into our memory banks. In the function of time, they are gone. But, in reality, they are still alive—on call from the unconscious mind, when needed to further our purpose in the earth.

The only actual time, then, that we ever have in which to act is this very present, fleeting, moment. And, while we speak, it is at once gone, and we have another moment to deal with. We must use each moment to determine our direction, our ideals, our goals. It is always highly important to make the choice for change and transformation—keeping our thoughts and actions positive in this moment—for it will eventually bring us to whatever goal we have chosen. It is just that simple.

The magic happens when we start to put this physiological puzzle together. We want to find out how all these important actions are related and how they coordinate and cooperate in bringing about a more balanced and harmonious life.

Building on the concepts explored in the first part of the book, let's look more definitively at how the power of choice plays such a dominant role in defining what really happens to our physical body. And then, let's see what it means to have an energy body.

We also need to examine the nervous system from a perspective that is based on function. Remember, we are working on the concept that the spirit is the life, the mind is the builder, and the physical is the result, so how our body functions is a necessary lesson.

Let's assume we chose to be born into the family that gave us life. That was done while we were still in the spiritual dimension. So part of our physiological makeup was given to us by our parents. We may have been given a physiological challenge, for the Universal Forces have a way of positioning us for the greatest spiritual growth that we are ready for—and may achieve—in this lifetime.

The emotional environment provided by our parents and perhaps also by our siblings influenced the formulation of our physiological balance (or imbalance). Our diet aided also in directing the activity of our internal workings. One can begin to see that there are many factors in operation from intrauterine life on through the formative years and beyond.

Why were we created like this? Why do we have five senses, a head, a body with two arms and two legs, an ability to maintain life through our different life support systems, and the ability to think, choose, and even tell a good joke?

Asking a question like this presupposes that I believe that we were, indeed, created. We didn't just happen. Evolution is not the answer, either, although there was a form that developed on the earth through that process which predated the creation of the human form.

These things seem logical to me, given that each of us on this planet Earth is an eternal being, a dweller in a sense on two planes of existence. The Cayce story of creation and the beginning of man's experiences in the earth is unique. As Cayce saw it, there was first the development of a form through the process of evolution that became the model for the later creation of the present configuration of man in the earth. Much of this information is too complex to be part of this book. Those interested in that kind of research can study it in the original Cayce readings.

But first we must recognize that we are truly energy beings. We are composed of atoms, put together in specific ways that are still mysterious for most of us. When atoms are broken down, energy is released. That's a known fact, isn't it? So, when we are dealing with the physical body, we are working with an energy being. An atom is defined as the smallest part of an element that is capable of entering into a chemical reaction. The nucleus is positively charged and the electrons carry a negative electrical charge. We need always to keep in mind that the entire body, then, is electrical in nature. And, in following the suggestions from the Cayce readings, we understand that the nature of the manifestation of God is electricity or electronic. Electricity is not God, but is rather the manifestation of God. An important point to remember.

The earth was created first as a habitation for man. Then God created the human form so we could in turn make a place for ourselves on the earth. It is important that we recall and keep in perspective that we existed prior to the earth's beginning.

After earth was ready for man, the human being had to have the ability to eat and drink, to protect himself and handle his environment creatively, to sustain life within his body and procreate the species. God gave life itself, in the form of what we call spirit, to man. But the rest of this creature we generically call "man" had to be able to manifest activity on the earth, had to *do* things with his body, using that essence of spirit, which not only created, but also sustained life in the organism. That's where the rest of the physical body comes into consideration.

Regarding man's advent into the earth the Cayce readings say: We saw the earth, and we liked it. Then we moved into this dimension. But it is never that simple to explain our entrance, for we usually think of ourselves as physical human beings born of the union of a mother and father. We must learn to accept the theory that we were spiritual entities first.

Our origin, then, defines the nature of our destiny, for we were created in God's image. And our end point—our destiny—is to be ourselves, yet to be one with the Creative Energies that brought both the worlds and us into existence.

Apparently the earth is an excellent place to meet the situations and the individuals who will, in turn, let us meet ourselves. With our understanding that God is love, we see that our way out of this dimension—the "meeting" of ourselves—is simply to learn how to love one another. We have our beginning in the consciousness of love—and we must in turn have our departure, finally, from this sphere as we learn that nature of the Divine, and live it in our lives. All these experiences lead us to understand that we are constantly on a journey which we call an adventure in consciousness.

That journey has taken us through many past incarnations in the earth, and undoubtedly will carry us forward through other earth experiences again and again and again, until we gain the oneness by simply learning how to love God and our fellow man, and then doing it.

When I was in medical school, Starling's textbook *Principles of Human Physiology* was our source of understanding the manner in which our bodies function. The description of our cerebrospinal nervous system is almost poetic. The description of the afferent electrical flow (impulses toward the brain) and the efferent flow (away from the brain) yields the following concept of consciousness:

"The states of consciousness glide continually from moment to moment in an unbroken stream of experience, consisting of a sharper focal content with a fringe of slighter definition, and leaving behind it a trace which we know as memory. By a process of attention we can single out parts of the stream of consciousness for closer focusing.

"There seems but little doubt that our conscious experiences are the result of complex integrations of sensory impressions, which are assessed by being checked and compared with traces of previous experiences" (page 332).

Cayce's viewpoint of consciousness differs from Starling's in that in Cayce's work the awarenesses that Starling writes about are components of the ongoing spiritual entity, and simply work through the physical body to make it aware of itself in this material dimension.

My understanding of Cayce's point of view as I integrated it with my own experiences and what I have learned about the human body might be stated like this: My body is a manifestation of my spiritual reality which might be called the soul-self. My body is also equipped with the sensory organs that allow me to experience this earthly dimension. These organs are properly grouped together into a functioning unit—the sensory nervous system.

While modern medicine places all parts of the nervous system except the brain and spinal cord in the peripheral nervous system, and the brain, along with the spinal cord, in the central nervous system, function is more important to our look at the mind/body/spirit connection than structure, for it is the normal function of different parts of the nervous system that allows the spiritual being to live purposefully in the earth plane.

My cerebrospinal nervous system, for example, allows me to be active in the earth dimension, to do things, to use my legs, my arms, my voice, and my bones and muscles to accomplish creative and helpful deeds.

The organs of my body, the systems that coordinate the work of the organs and the neuromuscular activities, everything that supports and maintains life in the body is under the control and direction of the autonomic nervous system. And the autonomic is the domain of the unconscious mind with all its memories of present and past lives. We might show these relationships as seen in Table 2.

Cerebrospinal	*Autonomic*	*Sensory*
We *do* things on earth	Life support Health/illness are created here.	We become aware of where we are
Conscious Mind	Unconscious Mind	Awareness

TABLE 2. THE 3 NERVOUS SYSTEMS.

All three of these nervous systems allow the human body—when it is functioning at a normal level—to experience consciousness. And the level of consciousness is finally determined by the degree to which the physical and mental bodies are attuned to the Creative Forces, or God.

There are feedback mechanisms in both the cerebrospinal and autonomic nervous systems, of course, which enable them to function and keep our systems in order. And it might be well to point out that our senses grasp information as it travels to our conscious awareness, but always impart information to the areas of the autonomic systems, which does not touch the conscious awareness, but is stored in memory for later retrieval, through recall, perhaps, or with the aid of hypnosis, visualization, or the meditative state. We are all much more totally aware than we ordinarily think we are, but much of it is unconscious, and is directed to that part of the nervous system where the unconscious mind is king.

The nervous system that keeps our organs and systems working together—or in a disturbed manner—is the autonomic. It is so named because it has an autonomy of its own, a rule that comes about without our conscious minds really being aware of its actions.

We were also intended to be active doing things here on the earth. Without taking action, buildings and roads are not built, inventions are not created, governments are not formed, foods not grown and harvested, and we ourselves would be unable to care for ourselves, or even think of helping others. These things come into being through the supervision and direction of the cerebrospinal nervous system. The brain monitors and is the headquarters for our conscious actions. Thus moving our bones and muscles along and enabling us to win Olympic medals or drive a car.

The third nervous system is rather far-flung in the body. It is not generally recognized as a system, yet it performs a most valuable task. It allows us to see, to hear a loved one's voice, to feel the touch of a hand, to smell the coffee in the morning, and to taste the home cooking at Thanksgiving time. It is called the sensory nervous system, and in addition to the activities of the eyes, ears, nose, and taste buds, it controls the sensory organs of feeling in the skin. Those specially formed nervous system adaptations that bring the neural impulses from the organs of the senses to the brain are intricate, and necessary to our consciousness of being in this dimension.

With these three nervous systems working in cooperation with one another, coordinating the senses, the muscles and tendons, and the life-support organs and systems, there is health. We find these things happening most optimally in a baby born healthy to a healthy mother in a well-integrated family.

To look at the body, then, from a different perspective, we can understand that our conscious mind works for the most part through the cerebrospinal nervous system, while the unconscious finds its activity in the autonomic. The two make up what we call our total mind—the conscious and the unconscious—and our senses allow us to be aware of our environment.

Most of the time when we try to understand the relationship

between our minds and our bodies, we have the idea that we are in control of everything we do. We get up out of bed in the morning when we want to, with alarm clock or not; we comb or brush our hair; we eat and drink our breakfast; we use the telephone; we drive a car; we do our daily work; we are businesslike or friendly, or both, and we do all these things by choice, and can do them consciously, when we want to.

A closer look, however, demonstrates something quite the opposite. We are not truly guiding or directing our destinies. There are a number of functions in these bodies of ours that are totally uncontrolled by the conscious mind, that progress sometimes in spite of what we consciously want them to do.

How can we, for instance, direct the manner in which the food that we eat for breakfast is to be digested? How can we consciously set up peristaltic waves in the intestinal tract? And how can we tell our heart to beat, or how often? Yet all these functions are controlled by autonomic directive. Involuntary control, we call it, but it acts much like the program of a computer. Once it's told how to do its job—and most of this comes through genetic control of intrauterine development—the control and the coordination take place. That's the purpose, the job description, of the autonomic nervous system. It truly has autonomy. But we must remember, too, that this autonomy can be changed by higher directive, as the conscious mind takes steps to reprogram the autonomic by whatever means it chooses.

It is generally understood that the forerunner of this complicated system of unconscious control is found in the ganglionated nervous system of the lower vertebrates. It is necessary for all living creatures to have life control installed in their bodies in order that they continue to exist in a living state.

When we make the leap from the lower vertebrates to single-celled creatures that live in water, or perhaps inside the structure of the human body, we experience a bit of a shock. These single-celled creatures (like the lymphocyte in the bloodstream) are able to find their way through their respective habitats when they have neither sensory organs nor nervous systems. Yet they move around between islands of cancer tissue, for example, destroying them before they themselves might be destroyed. An excellent movie of a lymphocyte in action is available from the American Cancer Society. Called *The Embattled Cell*, the movie shows the lymphocyte shaping itself like an arrowhead to penetrate the wall of a cancer cell directly above its nucleus. It pushes and pushes, until it gains entry into the cell. And we believe that once the lymphocyte enters the cancer, it destroys it.

When lymphocytes are not at war fighting the cancer that may be present, they seek our cells that need rebuilding, or regeneration. It appears that even the lymphocyte has consciousness of its own and performs its mission for the general good of the body, as it apparently has been instructed to do.

The human body, with its many parts, must with its consciousness coordinate even cellular function and give its diverse members their instructions and create the proper programs to help them out.

That we are so complex is understandable when we recognize that we are all motivated by the spirit of the Creative Source, and we have minds that take that Force and build the results that we find in our physical bodies. We have an even finer body—our permanent soul-body, and the one in which we experience the periods between incarnations, as well as the time spent here on the planet earth. All of us have this less dense body, and all of us will one day remember our glorious origin and look forward to an even more wonderful destiny.

Another way to look at this so-called uncontrolled nervous system which we know as the autonomic is to look at how it brings about its activities. All instruction travels through the separate parts of the far-flung system by means of nerve impulses. These impulses are electrical and carry messages, depending on what instructions are needed. Cayce had much to say about the electrical nature of man. Two short quotes illustrate his position on the matter:

For, as the very forces of the bodily functionings are electrical in their activity, the very action of assimilation and distribution of assimilated forces is in the physical body an active force of the very LOW yet very high VIBRATORY forces themselves. ⁴⁷⁰⁻²²

*Whatever electricity is to man, that's what the power of God is. Man may in the material world use God-force, God-power or electricity . . .*³⁶¹⁸⁻¹

The autonomic nervous system, in its electrical nature and activity, is composed of two parts—the sympathetic and the parasympathetic. They are generally regarded as working antagonistically, one sending out information to relax certain muscles, while the other acts to contract those same tissues. Rather than just disagreeing, however, they instead tend to augment each other by their reciprocity. Perhaps they respond like the dusk, stealing the light away from the day's vigorous activity. Both day and night are essential to life. Both the contraction and relaxation are indispensable to a peristaltic wave which moves digesting material down the intestinal tract.

The sympathetic nervous system—along with the adrenal gland activity—equips the body for its full muscular action, as in the offense or defense of a football team. One sees a football tackle working in the trenches against a formidable opposing line, all faculties alerted, all juices flowing to support the attack. Similarly, the sympathetic system is the dominant force in the body as it mobilizes all the existing bodily reserves for whatever emergency is present.

While the sympathetic rules the waking hours, the parasympathetic is usually dominant while one is asleep or resting after a heavy meal. Both systems are active to some extent, however, twenty-four hours a day.

When the body is at war—when one is arguing, beating a hasty retreat, under stress of any kind—all the parasympathetic activities in the intestinal tract, for instance, are markedly slowed down. Assimilation and peristalsis cease for the time being, as the blood supply and the nerve activity are channeled to the muscles and tendons.

But, when things are quiet and the body is prepared to eat its dinner in a friendly environment, the parasympathetic acts in fine, definitive neurological impulses. It plays its symphony in the intestinal tract, in a descending crescendo to cause the gut to contract in a wave-like fashion, much as one would see if he were to take a long, well-oiled balloon filled with water and squeeze it from one end toward the other. That is how food, to serve the body, is moved through the digestive tract in the process of assimilation and elimination.

While this finely tuned activity of the parasympathetic is progressing, the sympathetic must act also, much as two dancers taking part in a dance—one leading for a spell, then acquiescing. That's how these two systems work together, and the dance of life is going on every moment of our lives. For never is one entirely inactive.

How do these systems know when to take the lead in the dance? It has to have been learned with input—as in a computer—over the ages, as animals evolved, as man evolved, or as Cayce put it, "Matter began its ascent in the various forms of physical evolution in the mind of God" (262-99).

The parasympathetic portion of the autonomic system had the responsibility of creating acid in the stomach, in order that food would be properly digested. When the sympathetic activity—exercise, etc.—is slighted and the worries and anxieties of the body become dominant, too much acid is created, and the beginnings of an ulcer appear.

It is safe to say that there is no illness of the human body that does not involve some manner of improper function of the autonomic nervous system, either in its control of or relationship with other parts of the nervous system, or in its ability to coordinate the functions of the organs of the body.

Part of the healing process, then, in long-standing difficulties especially, must involve correction of the problem located somewhere in the autonomic nervous system. This is obviously quite difficult to accomplish, because we need to recognize first that these neurological impulses are manifestations of Creative Forces that have been misused by us in some manner. The result, since it is always a matter of consciousness, is an imbalance or an incoordination or a lack of cooperation within the areas of the body that give us life.

To understand this nervous system a bit more clearly, it should be noted that autonomic nerve fibers directed to many parts of the body most often are found traveling on the outer walls of the arteries and arterioles until they reach their destination. This places them in close contact with the blood supply to all the organs of the body—which, incidentally, they control—and puts them in intimate relationship with the body organs.

Within these human bodies of ours reside other forces that direct or lead these life-support systems and organs. Cayce liked to use the term "forces," because he indicated that it was the Life Force itself that gave each cell, each atom, the ability to do what it really needed to do. And, always, there was a function each was intended to fulfill.

To group these "forces" so they make sense from a functional point of view may be arbitrary, but function is what we are searching for from these organs and systems and not just an anatomical structure. The function must be associated with consciousness, for that is what brought us to the earth in search of a fulfilled purpose, as expressed in Diagram 5.

In Diagram 5, one's lifestyle, environment, and heredity are all shown to exert an influence on the body physiology. Suppose we were to be a guest at a meeting and we learned—too late—that the meeting was to be held in a smoke-filled room. There are at least three kinds of responses that could be brought about in the body.

First, we might act—decide consciously—to leave the room.

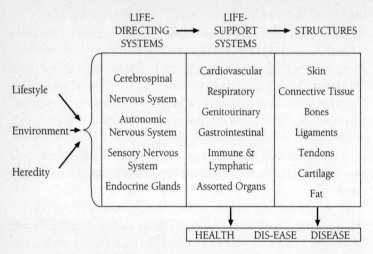

DIAGRAM 5. INFLUENCING THE BODY PHYSIOLOGY.

That involves the cerebrospinal nervous system. Before that, however, we would need to sense the situation, to become aware of it. The sensory nervous system performs that function and brings it to our consciousness, which then puts our body into action.

Second, the autonomic nervous system brings about a *reaction*. It might be that we have been very sensitive to smoke for years, and entering the room causes a nausea and instant headache—a physiological allergic reaction, and a very real problem, arising from an unconscious reaction mediated by the autonomic nervous system and those organs it controls.

The same situation—entering the smoke-filled room—could bring about a third response—a feeling of anger about anyone who would take us into a place like that when we are severely sensitive to smoke. The endocrine system—more specifically, the adrenal glands—is the arena where such feelings as anger reside and create their effects.

Thus, simply from a single environmental setting, (1) our senses may detect a problem; (2) a strong emotion might surface,

(3) an observable physiological set of reactions could come about, and (4) a conscious act might result.

Another environment might be experienced by one who is sensitive to abnormal electromagnetic fields and lives in a house built underneath high-tension electrical lines. Or, perhaps, in a cold or muggy climate, when one has respiratory problems to contend with. Or the hot desert, where pollens create unbearable allergies. The "environment" might even be living with a mother-in-law, or a sister, a brother, a spouse, when there is true enmity between the parties involved and you are trying to get along together under one roof.

Heredity, on the other hand, supplies us with another set of circumstances. We are given a complete new set of genetic coding when we are conceived in our mother's womb, something we did not consciously move into, as we might have a smoke-filled room. Yet at a level of choice that exists prior to our birth, we had the ability to choose and exercised it in order to enter a life path that would give us opportunities with individuals that we perhaps had been with before, and experiences that could help us on our path to our soul growth and eventual destiny. So birth is indeed also a choice that we have made, and this becomes our heredity.

We are given a set of organs and systems, of feelings that seem natural to us, of reactions that are the result of what we have chosen, and a physical body that allows us to take action. These circumstances affect the endocrine system, the autonomic nervous system, and the cerebrospinal system, but this time we don't need the senses to recognize the situation. We live with the circumstances as "normal" for each of us, conditions which we have chosen.

We may have acquired a childhood hereditary disease, and tend to think it was our parents' fault—all the time knowing at a deep unconscious level that we chose it before we were even born. Or we may be short in stature, and are frustrated because we are not tall. We may have a frail constitution, when it would be better to our way of thinking to be robust.

All these things generate distresses, worries, or other bothersome emotions. They in turn influence the life-support systems which take on the appearance of an orchestration of authorities, at a strictly unconscious level of function, creating a disequilibrium, a lack of coordination, which sooner or later spells dis-ease, and eventually disease if not corrected.

We consciously choose our lifestyles, although sometimes we do not acknowledge it or really believe it. And, as with the environment and heredity, our chosen lifestyles either aid or detract from the level of health we might enjoy.

Do you exercise regularly, for instance? What is your diet like—is it constructive and helpful to your body? Do you take enough rest and recreation to keep a healthy balance within your body? Is your work something you feel excited about every morning when you report at your workstation? Do you handle your job or does your job take control in your life? Is there any abuse of substances—drugs, alcohol, medications, cigarettes, food, and so on—in your personal history? How have you chosen to handle emotional situations? Do you meditate and pray regularly?

Emotional patterns we have chosen and exercised into habit patterns—whether they be large or small—influence the entire body, through the hormones that our endocrine glands distribute throughout the body via the circulatory system. Anger, for instance, originating from the adrenal glands, sends its messages through the bloodstream in the form of adrenaline and cortisone. At the same time, the neurological portion of the adrenals flashes its story instantly to all parts of the body by way of the extensive outreaches of the sympathetic portion of the autonomic nervous system.

All major glandular centers—like the adrenals—are neurohormonal transducers, acting on the body through nerve impulses and hormones, the latter distributed through circulation. These glands have the ability to translate neurological information into hormonal output.

Think about what happens when you get angry at the dinner table. A whole set of responses alerts the physical body for combat, strengthens the blood supply to the extremities, and essentially stops all activities designed to handle and properly digest and assimilate the food you might be eating. Ulcers, indigestion, digestive disorders of all kinds can come about when the rules of good eating are not followed. This is one good reason to enliven mealtimes with peace and joy, producing harmony instead of conflict. This will make you happier and healthier, for when one creates constructive, health-producing lifestyle patterns, all the physiological processes benefit and work toward maintaining and enhancing the general health of the body.

It's most helpful, then, to understand that our conscious mind acts; our unconscious mind reacts; our sensory organs perceive; and our endocrine organs feel. They all work together in a blending, an integration of influences that impels the other organs and systems. Thus all the life-support systems and organs are in reality dependent upon and directed by this blending and integration of authorities.

Within the bounds of the systems, the individual consciousness of the organs must in turn create a combining, an adjustment, a harmonizing of their awareness which emerge as a force that creates health, dis-ease, or disease. Oversimplified, it is true, but this kind of thing is real and active as the body continues to live and become part of an individual's search for purpose in the earth.

The structure of the body is not to be left out of our study, however. The bony parts; the muscles, tendons, and ligaments; the fat and connective tissues; and the skin (protecting and covering the body) all give us the substance that makes for strength, motion, and the physical assets that allow us to experience coordination and cooperation in the living activities of the human being.

There is considerable overlapping that needs to be acknowledged, and an anatomist or a physiologist would find much to
criticize in the above perspective of how things are in the human
body. However, in simplifying the body in a way that allows for
the overlapping, influencing, and coordinating of different functions or forces—as Cayce might call them—our definitions serve
a good purpose, as we further our understanding of the body, how
it functions internally, and how a variety of forces influence its
working parts, giving us an opportunity to create health instead of
disease.

It is always helpful to think in terms of living structures working either in cooperation with their neighboring organs or in conflict. For wars and arguments or love and friendship in the world
around us are like those found within the living body: They create the fruit of their labor outside the body—or within.

CHAPTER 10

Physiology and Healing

The gridiron is where football comes to life, whether you like football or not. The tennis court is the site of another kind of action, another game. Healing the body is still a different kind of a contest—undoubtedly far more important—but still one that calls for action—a war, in a sense, between those forces that would destroy and those that would build up the body and bring healing.

Every human being seeking healing of the body finds the real action in this game coming about within those functioning organs and systems inside his body, trying to keep the body alive and working. For they are the players in this game, acting out their part in this inner drama. And they always do their part most honorably and consistently, as long as they are working together as a team, cooperating in bringing about health-producing results. It is within the organs and systems that these forces of good and evil find their battleground. The liver, for instance, manages to serve the entire body as it lives out its knowledge of the body's divine origin. At the same time, toxins circulating in the bloodstream do their best to create havoc in the tissues of the liver. But its title as the great detoxifier becomes justified in its success while destroying the toxins.

It is when the physiological organs and systems of the body

function normally that health is truly born. The beginnings of all illnesses are found when malfunction of that physiology occurs. These disruptions then must be overcome and a reasonable balance restored in these areas before health can truly exist in the body as a whole. Where turmoil has created confusion or unsettling conditions, cooperation and balance must be restored. With a bit of help from outside, perhaps, the cooperation can be enhanced, and health once again comes into being.

Nothing in the healing process is more important to understand than the functioning physiology of the body, and how various forces and energies influence the workings. And probably no area is appreciated less adequately today among all health care practitioners and its key position in health and disease.

Medical training still orients the student to a diagnosis as the prime goal to be sought when a patient is presented with an illness. Unless a diagnosis is made, often little can be done. Treatment, when available, most frequently is directed at eliminating the illness or offending organ, as in removing a chronically infected tonsil, or using a drug to lower an elevated blood pressure. Frequently a gall bladder is removed, or an appendix, or a uterus to "help" a menopausal woman.

Attention is given in the medical format to the end result of an illness, rather than to the process that started it at some point in time, maybe weeks or months, or even years, ago. For there are forces that create abnormal functioning in the physiology of the body, and which, if allowed to continue, will eventually create a condition that has a group of symptoms and a name. And, lo, a diagnosis is born.

The Edgar Cayce readings, however, point us toward recognizing illness as a process from the very beginning until the disease can be diagnosed. The process of becoming ill takes time, but intervention can begin at any point along that time-scale, and needs only to change the course of events in order to be successful. Frequently, healing can happen before major procedures are required. In such an instance, the healing of the body may not be understood as correction of a cystitis, perhaps, because the problem was overcome and the body balanced before enough symptoms emerged to allow one to identify the problem as cystitis.

Simple procedures, such as a good night's rest, or just a family argument being set at rest, can bring about balance in the body to institute health once again.

Healing, then, may come about in a variety of ways, but Edgar Cayce said that the consciousness of the individual was the primary determining factor. Every cell, every organ, even every atom has consciousness. Each part of God's world, down to its molecular structure, is aware of its origin and its destiny.

Perhaps this is why I am captivated by the variety of illnesses that respond to very simple remedies. It may be that the remedy has a vibratory nature which will bring about new awarenesses to the cell or the organ. For consciousness is still what we are looking at when we consider healing.

It was some time ago that a man wrote to me of his experience with castor oil. It has always been remarkable to me how many problems respond with health and healing when the oil of the lowly castor bean is applied to the body. Castor oil can cleanse the body when taken orally—many of us can remember becoming acutely aware of that. If cleansing is its consciousness, then it can cleanse wherever it is applied. And cleansing often allows cellular structures to regenerate themselves.

This man's letter told how he had suffered with a condition usually corrected only by surgery—a hernia. He wore a standard hernia belt on his left lower abdomen, then the same condition showed up on the right side, so he switched to a double hernia belt. Eventually he had to undergo surgery on the right side.

For the next two years, he continued wearing the appliance, but he started to massage both areas with hot castor oil, using a rotary motion—clockwise on the left, counterclockwise on the right. The oil was liberally applied during the massage and perhaps two to three tablespoons were absorbed by the body. Within several months the condition greatly improved, and in several more months cleared up. The combination of the oil, massage, and a tremendously positive attitude aided the man's recovery.

Cayce found that balance and proper working of the body was, in many instances, dependent upon whether or not each organ and part was coordinating and cooperating with other parts, and whether toxins or products of metabolism were being removed promptly from the body.

In the instance of the individual who had a hernia, it could be postulated that the castor oil promoted the elimination of waste products from the cells located in the areas involved in the hernia, thus allowing the cells to function more normally, and accept the help of the immune system in rebuilding or regenerating that which was partially out of order.

Achieving a balance in the body systems requires an environment of cooperation and coordination of efforts. The most basic reference to balance I found in the Cayce readings describes what happens in the individual atoms of the body as healing comes about:

> As we have indicated, the body-physical is an atomic structure subject to the laws of its environment, its heredity, its SOUL development. The activity of healing, then, is to create or make a balance in the necessary units of the influence or force that is set in motion.[281-24]

If a balance is achieved between the eliminations and the assimilations, the promise found in the Cayce readings is that one can then live to any age desired. This kind of a balance is difficult to create. Look at the pastry section of the supermarket or at any pastry display. All sorts of goodies are there to tempt one to overindulge. When one succumbs to this kind of a situation, when his choices are not particularly constructive, then the body suffers.

I've often thought that eating too much of anything is much like what sometimes comes about when a naive young bachelor stocks his first kitchen. Never having shopped before, he buys twenty-five pounds of bananas. He likes bananas! After surviving abundantly on bananas for the next week, he surveys the pile of bananas still left in his kitchen and becomes despondent. He simply can't eat any more and the bananas are going bad. Not knowing to make banana bread, or pie (and overeat with that, too), he finally takes the rest of the now-spoiled bananas out to the compost pile or trash can. The young bachelor spent time, money, and energy bringing the bananas into the house, used what he could, and spent wasted time, energy, and money taking the remainder out of the house.

When we eat, we often consume more food than our bodies—no matter how hard they try—can properly use. Some of the food, of course, is turned into energy and utilized by the cells of the body to continue the life process. Some of the excess is built into the tissues of the body as fat, stored as energy for future use. But much of the food—like the bachelor's bananas—never finds a home or a real use in the body. This is what Cayce calls "refused forces," and they must be eliminated or they cause difficulty in the body itself, perhaps by acting as toxins, or by being put away where a lot of action takes place, as in a joint or muscles. This could be the beginning of arthritis.

The cells that have thrived because of the food offered the body continue the living process and produce hormones or other aids to the body. In the same manner, they produce waste products, like every living thing. These wastes are called metabolites and are the end products of cell metabolism. Cayce called them "used forces." Some cells also die, and the breakdown products add to the sum of the used forces.

It thus becomes more understandable that elimination is a vital function of the body. The kidneys, the liver, the intestinal tract, the skin, and the lungs are designed to fulfill these duties. Organs and systems do not perform normally when the blood supply furnished them is polluted, giving them as food substances little more than waste products—the used and refused forces, in Cayce's terminology.

There are only these four systems that provide elimination of waste products from the body. The liver, along with the bowel, constitutes one means of removing wastes. And we most often think of that, along with the kidneys and urinary system, to be the whole of the elimination process. This is not so, of course, for the skin—with its perspiration—is a very large organ and helps if given a chance through exercise, or anything that makes one sweat. And the lungs not only bring in food for the body through air, but also remove toxins and waste products from the bloodstream.

If one of these organs or systems is deficient, the others must help out by extending their capacity, until a healthy consciousness, a balance, and a more normal function can be restored to the unhealthy organ.

I've always felt that the inner portions of the body, the life-support systems, can function normally if we give them proper care, and if we are able to create a coordination among all these functions. Much as we would expect to happen in an organization or a family. And this means a coordination among the consciousnesses of the very cells and atoms making up the organs and systems concerned. We can have peace or war. The war brings destruction. Peace brings happiness and health.

If there truly is a type of consciousness even in the atom, as Cayce suggests, then there has to be communication. Communication leads to a relationship that brings about either a harmonious result or discord. So it would be expected that we try for a good relationship between the liver and the spleen, for instance, between the urinary tract and the kidneys, among the different parts of the heart and blood vessels, between the endocrine organs and the gastrointestinal tract, between the lungs and the spinal cord, and so on. All these entities do not exist in a vacuum, but rather as a unit seeking a oneness among all parts, directed toward the welfare of the body as a whole.

Taking these concepts into consideration, it becomes more and more important that we see coordination of our functioning human body as critical to the search for healing. And yet, the state of health might well be looked at simply as a physiological balance that mirrors the manner in which the body was created in the first place.

Psychoneuroimmunology is the study of the relationships found between the immune system and the human nervous system, the mind, the emotions, and that area—poorly defined in science today—known as the psyche or the soul. Scientific circles would say that "psyche" refers to the mind, as in psychology. However, the dictionary definition shows it to be the human soul, spirit, or mind. Until rather recently, the immune system was not considered to be related to the nervous system, and certainly not to the mind or the emotions, or the spiritual reality.

Today, however, these ideas have come of age, and the study draws the attention of psychiatrists, endocrinologists, and even the molecular biologists. Some of the more radical of these people believe that there is no state of mind that is not faithfully reflected by a state or level of immune function.

And it has been discovered that immune responses can be learned. Visualization brings changes in the immune system's ability to respond. Apathy toward and dynamic refusal to accept cancer bring about diametrically opposed responses in the body, as seen in the number of lymphocytes, whose job is to kill cancer cells. And it has been reported from many circles that meditation or prayer affects the degree of immune response to a variety of illnesses.

When one searches out the studies being done throughout the world today, it becomes evident that meditation, attitudes, emotional patterns, thoughts held by the mind, the nervous system, and the immune system are all closely interrelated. Facial expressions have even been shown to produce the physiological changes that one would expect from the acting out of the emotions suggested by that same expression—most likely because these same emotions are to be found inside the body, although the individual harboring them may not even be aware that they are being shown on the face to the public.

Thus it is helpful always to your immune system to smile, harmful to frown; helpful to believe, harmful to discredit; helpful to be happy, harmful to be sad. Perhaps, then, it should not seem unusual for a spouse to die of a broken heart (immune system failure) when a loving partner dies suddenly.

Seeing the thymus as master of the immune system, we need to recognize it also as metaphysically controlling the sensitive feelings centered around the chest and the breasts and even the heart. And when a heartache like the loss of a loved one comes about, that area hurts. Then the ability of the thymus to act normally is depressed, and the body's defenses are, to a certain extent, lost. The heart aches, and sometimes the heart stops.

Evaluating the immune system is not a simple matter. When it is considered metaphysically, however, the thymus and its activities can be assessed more easily by the emotional tone and lifestyle of the individual. But changes in the internal functioning of the body are often indicative of troubles, whether they occur in the immune system or in the control of the acid/alkaline balance in the body. In a reading given by Cayce for an individual who was suffering with "acidity," he offered these interesting comments that relate the use of iodine to other endocrine glands of the body as well as the acid/alkaline balance, and the circulation of the lymph. As Cayce surveyed the human body, he saw very intricate and important relationships existing. This is the reading extract:

> One drop of Atomidine in half a glass of water before the morning meal, and the next day three drops of Glyco-Thymoline in water before retiring. . . . Alternate these . . . and within a few weeks the acidity of the system will be changed, and also the vibrations through the glandular forces that control the lymph circulation in alimentary canal as well as organs of the pelvis . . . The Atomidine acts as a gland purifier—causing especially the thyroids and the glands of the stomach, particularly the pyloric portion of the stomach and throughout the duodenum, to change in the form of secretions thrown off—and this affects directly the circulation.[3104-1]

The early Edgar Cayce readings provided information for the formulation of the substance known as Atomidine. It is basically an iodine preparation. The readings suggested Atomidine or sometimes other forms of iodine as a therapeutic measure for quite a variety of ailments.

Iodine, it seems, is a vital element in the makeup of the human body. The readings tell us that iodine is essential to the process of building new cells, or cell division. One reading discusses what Cayce was able to see of the activity of Atomidine when taken inside the body.

> *The Atomidine—that is activative in the glands, especially the thyroid, the adrenal and all the ductless activities through the atomic forces in iodine, the one basic force with potash—makes for a balance throughout the functionings of the body itself.* 636-1

Potash, chemically, is potassium carbonate (K_2CO_3), closely related to potassium bicarbonate ($KHCO_3$), which is used to neutralize acid of the stomach and to treat acid-base imbalance elsewhere in the body. In the readings, sodium bicarbonate, as well as Glyco-Thymoline, an alkaline mouthwash which contains sodium bicarbonate, are also used to normalize acid-alkaline imbalances.

When discussing the acidity or alkalinity of a liquid or a tissue of the body, it should be noted that the hydrogen ion concentration—the pH value—is always involved. The neutral point, where a solution would be neither acid nor alkaline, is pH 7. Increasing acidity is expressed as a number less than 7 and increasing alkalinity as a number greater than 7. Maximum acidity is pH 0, and maximum alkalinity is pH 14. (Because each unit on the scale represents a logarithm, there is a tenfold difference between each unit.)

Where does this come into consideration? Gastric juice, for instance, usually ranges from pH 1.0 to 5.0. The blood plasma has a pH that hovers close to 7.35. All tissues of the body have their individual pH values—some low and some rather high. When the pH of any particular part of the body becomes chronically unbalanced, one can expect the beginning of a disorder which may proceed to become a disease process.

The bloodstream is mandated by the mind of the autonomic nervous system to maintain a rather rigidly controlled pH level. This is very important to the overall health of the body. Alkalosis or acidosis in the bloodstream can be serious trouble, sometimes needing emergency medical care.

Thus, when any influence tends to make the body over-acid, for instance, the effect is distributed by the bloodstream to another part of the body, leaving the blood with a still well-regulated pH. The lymphatics are chosen as the initial carrier of the excess chemicals that bring about a slightly lowered pH and an accompanying relative acidosis, or acidity, as Cayce called it.

The lymphatics throughout the body normally have a slightly higher—or more alkaline—pH than the bloodstream. And it needs to be remembered that the immune system, directed by the thymus gland, includes the tonsils, adenoids, spleen, liver, appendix, Peyer's Patches (in the intestines), lymph nodes throughout the body and the entire complex of lymphatics. Thus, when the pH of the lymphatics is depressed, as described in the last paragraph, there is a real depression of the normal function of the entire immune system.

The lymphocytes created in the lymph nodes and other sites of lymphatic tissue are undoubtedly happier in an alkaline state than in one more acid. Anything in one's lifestyle, then, that would create acidity in the body to be absorbed and distributed through the bloodstream would at once bring about an unfavorable medium in which the lymphocytes would be born or perform in their defensive activity. In other words we can always be active in choosing a good alkaline reacting diet or a lifestyle which would bring about a happy heart and a more normal and slightly alkaline pH level.

The very small arterial capillaries that bring food to the cells of the body are only one cell distant from the beginnings of the lymphatic stream. For the cell takes food and fluid from the bloodstream and eliminates its products, whether wastes or hormones, into the intercellular spaces, which become the origin of the lymphatic stream, ending up finally as the thoracic duct, which in turn empties into the vena cava just prior to its entrance into the heart.

In Cayce's opinion, it takes very minimal changes in the acid-base balance to bring about not only a more normal pH level, but also a vibratory change in the glands that control the lymph circulation in the GI tract and the organs of the pelvis, among other places. This human body is a remarkable organism. It doesn't take much to redirect the course of health. An emotional upset can create illness—and a few drops of Glyco-Thymoline can bring back a state of health.

Some years ago, I was asked to see an infant that some A.R.E. parents brought to Virginia Beach for a seminar. The child was ill, running a fever, but no other findings were present except a slightly reddened throat. It was late at night and no druggists were open and I had no medicines. The parents did have some Glyco-Thymoline, however. They were instructed to give their son three or four drops in a little water at once, and repeat it every few hours through the night.

The child fell asleep shortly after the second treatment and didn't wake up all night long. In the morning, he was afebrile and had no further trouble the rest of the week. This experience taught me that gentle aid to the body often is all that is needed. I was prepared to understand why Cayce said time after time that if one were to keep a slightly alkaline balance in his body, he would never catch cold. I've tested that statement numerous times and find that it works.

There are few chronic problems of the elderly woman more distressing than osteoporosis, a progressive loss of calcium in the bone structures that leads to multiple fractures and subsequent disability. Many clinical efforts have been mobilized to help prevent or correct this condition. One that has been used for years at the A.R.E. Clinic is the combination of calcium, taken by mouth, and the female hormones, in small dosages.

It has long been thought that menopause (the decrease in the level of estrogen in the circulating blood) was a major causative factor in osteoporosis. Recent studies have indicated that the cause may, indeed, be associated with menopause, but may lie more directly within a change in body acid-base balance that causes more calcium to be lost through the kidneys, and then replaced in the bloodstream from the bone itself. This, in turn, causes the bone to become more fragile, more easily fractured, and more generally to be recognized as osteoporotic in nature.

A paper by Josephine Lutz, Ph.D., published in the February 1984 issue of the *American Journal of Clinical Nutrition*, demonstrated that urinary calcium increased dramatically when women of different ages were given an increased ingestion of an acid-ash diet. Protein intake was increased from a sixteen-day stable 44 gm. level to 102 gm. for fourteen days. (The main source of the protein was turkey roll or ground round steak.) The increase in protein intake raises the body's acid state. Then, for the next ten days, a teaspoon (5.85 gm.) of sodium bicarbonate was added, divided into three small doses each day. With the alkalinization of the bloodstream and subsequently the urinary stream, the calcium loss was markedly decreased, leaving the body in a positive, rather than a negative, calcium balance.

Researchers have postulated that the increased acidity of a diet may be the major factor in creating osteoporosis, in a sense bleeding calcium out of the bone to equalize the body otherwise and thus creating the loss of calcium from the bloodstream into the urine.

The basic diet suggested in the Edgar Cayce readings would seem to be a major corrective factor in preventing this problem in the postmenopausal woman. Or in any woman, for that matter. The diet is low in protein, high in alkaline-ash foods such as vegetables and fruits, avoids fried foods and white flour and white sugar products, and emphasizes fish, fowl, or lamb for protein sources.

The Lutz research has gone for the most part unnoticed among those who are working with osteoporosis, but logic says that the simple addition of baking soda in small doses would be helpful for those who already have the osteoporotic problem, and anything leading to a gentle or slightly alkaline balance in the body tissues would be most beneficial.

The pH of any given body can be disturbed either toward the acid or the alkaline side by the simple living process. A night's sleep lost can be just as upsetting as a supervisor's harsh criticism. If one misuses his dietary program, the same thing can happen—a change in the pH can come about. Lack of exercise, bad news, attitudes one chooses to adopt that are not consistent with one's ideals and soul direction—all these can bring about a change in the cells of the body, in the organs and in the systems, which starts the process of illness, or makes it worse, simply by lowering the body pH, and depressing the immune system and its activity.

A positive frame of mind prior to surgery can make a major difference in the success of the procedure and the postsurgical course. And simply by adopting a way of life, an attitude, that reassures us that all is well despite the appearances, we can produce for the immune system an environment that is healing. We are indeed wonderful human beings, and we have more control over our destiny than we would like to think.

The first clue that something is wrong in our bodies is most commonly an ache or pain. These feelings may not be taken seriously by the consciousness of the individual, but the feelings may not go away. Even if we choose to ignore the aches and pains, they are still there, and if not balanced out by aiding the body in one way or another, the disturbance can continue and become more serious as time passes.

It must be remembered that every serious illness has its apparently trivial beginning. The disturbance we call dis-ease, and the cause, can be as simple as one's lifestyle.

We need to remember that, potentially, all of us have the ability to search inside our bodies and know what is either going astray or keeping a balance. Edgar Cayce demonstrated this thousands of times—so frequently that we don't think of it as being unusual for him. But it's a bit difficult for us to do. In his deeply altered state of consciousness (some call it a trance), Cayce communicated with the unconscious mind of another person, gaining information from the awareness of that functioning autonomic nervous system that let him describe it in words: how one system might be suffering with a deficiency of energies from food; how the kidney, for instance, might be out of coordination with the liver; how the balance might be disturbed between the assimilations of the body and its eliminations.

What this lets us understand is that Cayce really didn't manufacture the information himself, but instead obtained it from the individual's own consciousness, where it was so subliminally planted that the subject could not reach it himself. We need to realize that all the information about how our bodies are functioning lies within our grasp. Even though it may be difficult to see, understand, or take hold of, it is still there. The problem is that our grasp has not yet developed sufficiently to make the information available to our conscious mind with any degree of ease. But the knowledge does lie within our own body consciousness! And that is indeed significant.

We need to develop our abilities to become more sensitive, more acutely aware of our bodies. For within the confines of our skin, in a very real sense, lie responses to all sorts of experiences we have encountered in this lifetime, plus a wealth of information from past lifetimes. We know how our functions would be performing if they were all healthy and coordinated—we know that, but we aren't yet able to be fully aware of it.

What do we look for, if we conscientiously seek this kind of understanding and patiently pursue the effort? What if we listen to what our body is saying and we check on minor symptoms before they become major? Certainly, this would involve more study than can be made available in the pages of this book. But we would surely avoid illnesses that would otherwise come about.

A reference such as *The Color Atlas of Human Anatomy* (edited by Vanio Vannini and Giuliana Pogliani, Beekman House, Crown, 1980) would be helpful. It was done originally in Italy, translated to English in 1980, and contains text and color drawings that present the human body graphically and dramatically. It is intended for the layman, but stimulates the imagination even of the professional. Being able to visualize what your body is like through the eye of the artist will give you an even greater appreciation of the wonders of how you are put together. There are, however, subjects that need to be pursued to establish a good basis for understanding what is going wrong.

When a portion of the body moves away from its normal pattern of life, we say it malfunctions. This can happen with any of the organs or systems, and it does. There are always reasons behind the obvious reason why the abnormal function comes about, but these reasons are sometimes difficult to perceive. Take the very first sign of a bout of influenza, for example. The body might ache a bit, and one wonders if it is from overactivity or perhaps from losing too much sleep. We just don't feel up to par. Sooner or later, we find out that it is the respiratory tract that has lost its integrity, and a virus has invaded. Later on, other organs and systems might become involved in the disease process.

Sometimes, on the other hand, the cause of a malfunction is quite apparent, as in hepatitis, when the sclera of the eyes become yellowed and the beginning of jaundice is found in the skin and in the palms of the hands. We know the liver is malfunctioning. If one is awakened during the night and needs urgently to empty his bladder, one does not need a textbook of medicine to understand that the kidneys or bladder are in trouble. A knowledge of the body along with a healthy dose of common sense will enable us to understand bodily functioning. But when does the question of therapy come into the picture? Cayce had much to say about treatment of the body, but this reading is particularly appropriate when considering restoration of normal function:

> In beginning, let this body—and all others for that matter—make sure of this: Unless it be for a removal of conditions that have become acute by neglect or other causes of the same nature, all curative forces must be from within self and are of the whole of a physical being; for the human anatomical body is as the working of a perfect whole of a piece of machinery, and that—kept in the proper working order—will perform the function of not only furnishing its own fuel for operation but supply that necessary for replenishing that fuel, would the body supply same with foods that will build in the system in proper proportions to that needed from within. [4999-1]

We need to keep in mind, then, that malfunctions do not come about except in relationship with the rest of the body, where all parts have a purpose and a working relationship with other parts.

Some years ago, in doing research with the Cayce readings, I became impressed with the frequent reference to "incoordinations." I thought it would be interesting to do a special study on this that Cayce saw to be so common in the ailing body. After my son, Bob, who was acting as my research associate, did a compilation of the readings where incoordination was mentioned, I saw the sheaf of papers with double or triple rows of numbers on them and decided the research could come later. There were several hundred references on just that subject.

In my mental pondering over this word, wondering why it was such a common concept, I uncovered an idea that made the definition more clear. If, for example, a receptionist in a medical office were to list next Tuesday's patient appointments on Wednesday's schedule by mistake, while the second receptionist were to go ahead and fill Tuesday's time slots—all those who were told to come on Tuesday, including those who were on Wednesday's books, would appear. And it would be havoc in the office.

This is an instance of incoordination between receptionist number one and number two. The body (in this instance, the office) would be coming down with a case of angina—not deadly, for sure—but needing a therapy program. In this instance, the remedy might simply be more adequate communication.

The body needs adequate communication as well. If there is a breakdown in communication between the autonomic and the cerebrospinal nervous systems, the body will malfunction and the organism will become ill. The liver and the kidneys need to work together to keep the health of the body in top shape. It's easy to give voice to this kind of concept, but it helps to recall that each cell, each organ, each system has a consciousness of its own, and normal function must arise out of adequate communication and devotion to duty.

An army also depends on such conditions. The general of an army does not tell his subordinates how to do their job—they know that and have learned it well. But the general does tell his colonels what he wants accomplished, and he knows it will be done. That's when the level of command takes over.

It's much like that inside the human body. Every organ, every system has its own job to perform, and given the help that is needed in the way of a richly supplied blood supply and the influence coming in loud and clear through the nervous systems, each will successfully fulfill its own destiny, working in a cooperative manner with other areas of consciousness in the body.

The diet, of course, plays an essential part in creating health or disease in our life-support systems, which are always working even while we sleep. But assimilation is far more than just choosing the food that we eat. All food must go through the digestive process, starting in the mouth as we let the saliva do its part while we chew our food. The stomach does its part, as do the bile, the liver, the gallbladder, and the pancreas. All parts of the upper intestinal tract have their duties along the way.

The assimilative activity does not stop there, however, for all food must then be taken into the lymph or bloodstream through the walls of the intestinal tract, changed even more, and then finally—whether taken through the liver or not—given to the circulatory system for distribution to the entire body. Perhaps you recall all this from high school Health.

Yet any part of that complex circuit that functions defectively can cause what we would call an illness or a disease. A classic case in point is the disease known as iron-deficiency anemia. One of my patients, a forty-five-year-old woman, had a hemoglobin of 9.3 gm. (Normal is more like 13 gm.) I had her start taking an iron preparation—Feosol—and she returned to our office six weeks later. Her hemoglobin was still 9.3, but she had in the meantime developed a skin rash. It is known that iron taken orally often does cause this condition, so I had her stop the iron.

I had been writing a book at that time dealing with the way in which Edgar Cayce recommended castor oil as a therapy in his readings. I asked my patient if she had ever taken castor oil as a child. She said, "Oh, lots of times! I never minded it at all." My objective was to cleanse the system of irritants to the skin and get rid of the rash. So I instructed the woman to take an ounce of castor oil that evening, and repeat it in four days.

Well, she did not show up again until six weeks later. I asked her why it took so long to report. She told me that she had been feeling so good since she started taking the castor oil every four days that she didn't think she needed to come back right away. Her rash, of course, was completely gone.

I checked her hemoglobin once more, and it was 13.1 gm., perfectly normal. She had stopped the iron supplement, which had not worked to improve her blood picture, yet when she took the castor oil her hemoglobin responded. There is no iron in castor oil, of course. So, I asked myself, what happened? The only answer I could come up with was that the castor oil cleansed the lining of the stomach and upper intestinal tract, and the cells all cheered—for now they could act normally, and take iron from the woman's natural diet. This is an example of cellular recovery, balance, and then normal function, which led me to understand that the body can be aided in some of the most unusual ways to return back to normal.

And when both elimination and assimilation are cooperating, and each doing its particular job well, we have what can be called a state of homeostasis, or a relative condition of health. In other words, the food is providing what is needed, elimination is taking away the used and refused forces—the body wastes—and the life-support systems are being given an excellent chance to function normally, in balance, and in coordination with other parts of the body.

Yet, both assimilation and elimination are more than their physical functions would lead one to believe. Both have symbolic importance, leading to a deeper understanding of one's true self, the feelings, the emotions, and the blocks that have often stopped the healing process.

It is said that Jesus told his disciples that what comes out of the mouth is more important than what goes in. The food entering the system is not as important as the words that issue forth from the heart and soul of the individual.

And we should realize that when we hold resentments and unspoken frustrations and angers inside ourselves, they build toward a physical demonstration of the inner person—constipation, for example. Often, of course, the problem that surfaces is more important than simple constipation, and can become life-threatening. But all these things might be called blocks or walls, fences or stones—something in the path we really want to avoid, but cannot. We are, in a true sense, imprisoned by our secret, deeply imbedded, destructive emotional patterns. Yet we need to remember that these prisons can be opened, these blocks can be removed, and these paths can be cleared of obstructions. It certainly is not simple, but an understanding of the mind/body/spirit connection is essential.

Perhaps the best way to understand the relationship of the mind, body, and spirit as they perform their duties inside our bodies is to start out with that realization once again that we are spiritual beings, fashioned in the image of the Creative Forces of the

Universe, and have our origin in a spiritual dimension. We are here in the earth trying to find our way back home.

If we take the perspective—as Cayce did—that electricity is the manifestation of God, and that we have that God Force active within ourselves, making possible every movement, every thought, every function, then it begins to make more sense that the power of choice can help our minds become more active as builders and bring about the cooperation and the coordination within that spells health and balance in our bodies.

We find that it is the consciousness of the cells and the organs themselves that makes it possible for the assimilation of food-stuffs and the elimination of those used and refused forces to work together, or to fail in their task to bring health to the body.

Yet we find that the choice of foods that we put into our bodies sometimes overrides the desire and consciousness of these organs in creating difficulties and an imbalance. And that choice is always available. So what we eat and how we care for our eliminations (I use eliminations to describe all four channels—the lungs, the skin, the kidneys, and the liver/intestinal tract) is up to us in our awakening consciousness. Cayce said many times that what we eat and what we think make us what we are.

The importance of the circulatory system in this process cannot be overrated either. It carries all that food to its appointed place, and the oxygen that is needed, particularly in the brain, where our thought processes originate. Life, we know, is present in every cell and atom of the body, but its survival in the earth plane of existence is dependent upon an adequate oxygen supply, for without oxygen, life leaves the body.

Our activities, such as exercise, recreation, and rest, as well as work, also affect the physiology of the body. The exercise keeps the tone of the body muscles and stimulates the intake of oxygen into the lungs and the circulation. Recreation satisfies the heart and the mind and balances the body as a whole in relationship to the work that we do—which is often the reason we are here on the earth. Work is that important. Rest allows the body to rebuild.

All the systems of the body are called on to perform, and they love it.

But it is our unconscious emotional tendencies, found for the most part in the endocrine glands, where past life memories are often stored, that have the most direct impact on our physiological processes. Fear and doubt, anger and frustrations bring about a substrate to our overall health. While Cayce did not always describe the direct connection neurologically, or through endocrine activities, he did relate emotions to consciousness, and to the state of the physical body. One reading told the story like this:

Q-4. Any spiritual advice?

A-4. Much has been given this body as respecting the mental and spiritual attitude, and that the attitude is reflected more in that in which the individual entity meets its problems with itself as well as with others. If there are the worries and aggravations, these worries and aggravations will reflect in the functioning of the organs of the central nerve and blood supply as well as in the sympathetic. Then know in whom ye believe and know He is able to keep that ye may commit unto Him against any experience. [338-9]

And he went on to say that it is the belief of the body that it will waste away with age or fear or the like that produces old age. The glands, of course, are directly related to the emotions. It's obvious from Cayce's perspective that consciousness brings about a balance within the physiological body and is a primary factor in the creation of health—or disease—and eventually illness. But we must also keep in mind that the consciousness of substances in nature such as castor oil, which God created, is there for us to use, too.

A friend of mine who is a general and peripheral vascular surgeon wrote me this letter: "About a year and a half ago, a good friend of mine in his thirties told me that during his coughing-up episodes (one or two every three to five minutes for the last several years) he would bring up some granular, soft nodules which when crushed revealed a foul odor. I obtained some and found that he had actinomycosis, fortunately without lung cavitation or systemic symptoms.

"I notified his family doctor, who had put him on penicillin for the last year and a half. He noted that his cough reduced slightly but he occasionally still brought up non–foul-smelling granules. I had had him try various Cayce remedies for other problems in the past, including the castor oil packs, so I had him apply a castor oil pack for half an hour to the front of his chest, then half an hour to the back on a daily basis for about five to six weeks. The cough that he had had for years is now gone."

Alleviation of such a cough certainly bodes well for suppression of infection with the actinomyces organism with castor oil, as transmitted through packs on the back and the front of his chest. This healing example is also a good indicator of that individual body's ability to resuscitate and reorganize itself, and bring about a valid healing response.

It may be that the vibration and touch of the oil called "the Palma Christi" in the Middle Ages carries with it a consciousness of its own that says to us, "Here's a bit of healing that you might use, if you choose!"

It now should be apparent why we develop an upset stomach after a particularly disagreeable argument with our spouse or our child, or one of our close friends. The adrenal glands have been too active, certainly, and if we have an upset stomach frequently enough, we are more apt to develop a serious affliction in that part of our body that the adrenal controls. An attitude of combativeness, an adversarial point of view, a lack of peace in one's consciousness will, in fact, create turmoil in the functioning body, and help shape the physiology of the body in a way that is not health-producing.

The turmoil inside, then, the problem in its essence, is that we are ill because we have not yet gained the consciousness of peace as a constant state of mind. I did a bit of research on peace as it is found in the Bible and also in the Cayce material. There are a multitude of references, but some are particularly pertinent to the turmoil inside our bodies that leads to illness, and how oneness with God creates peace within our own bodies, and subsequently a healing process.

Isaiah foresaw the coming of the Christ Child and called him, among other terms (Wonderful, Counselor, the Mighty God, the Everlasting Father), the Prince of Peace (Isaiah 9:6). And Paul wrote to the Christians of Philippi (4:7), "And the peace of God, which passeth all understanding, shall keep your hearts and minds through Christ Jesus."

Jesus told his disciples, "Peace I leave with you, my peace I give unto you" (John 14:27). And throughout the writings of Paul in the New Testament, peace is part of what we understand to be the fruits of the spirit, the manner in which the Creative Forces manifest love in the earth through people. We are channels of the God-Force here on the earth, whether we turn the power to our own desires (which we can do through our ability to choose) or whether we are clear purveyors of the love that God would have us experience.

In checking through the body of the Edgar Cayce readings, one of our clinic researchers discovered that peace is mentioned 1,317 times, which indicates that many individuals—most of whom were ill—were in need of peace as Cayce discussed it.

> For remember, it is only self ye are meeting that causes anxieties or any character of trouble. For thou hast been from the beginning. It is up to thee as to whether ye continue. The soul that sins shall be cut off—the soul that sins purposefully, that doesn't use the opportunities given by manifestations in life. And what is the law of the Lord? "Thou shalt love the Lord thy God with all thy mind, thy body, thy soul, and thy neighbor—thy brother, thy friend, thy foe—as thyself." The whole law is in this. Ye can apply it to this or that extent, but do apply it in the whole law if ye would be at peace with self and know the peace which passeth understanding to a materially minded individual or world. *4047-2*

Let's return to the instance where we find ourselves having arguments with a loved one that escalate to the point where they are serious and cause an upset stomach or ulcer. The arguments induce wars between the peaceful forces of the soul, and more combative, materialistic forces in the self, and these wars arise from those experiences given us from the outside. Too often, the attitudes that bring discord continue to be strengthened, making the resistance more powerful, and the battle is won, at least temporarily. Peace, then, departs from the landscape, which in this instance is a part of the functioning body. We call the outcome "stress" in the person who experiences the gastric hyperacidity. And, like it or not, stress comes about from a choice taken within the body.

Then, sometimes, we remember that everything in materiality is of the Creative Forces, brought about for our use and purposes, and we go at it again, trying to do that which brings peace to our being. Cayce said, in another reading, that

> just being kind, just being in that manner in which the fellow man is served day by day; and that the outcome of same is fellowship, patience, kindness, gentleness, brotherly love—these manifested in the experience . . . as a living example day by day . . .
>
> These should be, as has been indicated, the mental attitudes of the body, if there is to be had that which brings harmony, peace, understanding, and those things that make not afraid. 391-8

Harmony, balance, peace, understanding—all these are part of that life which, if manifested through oneself, brings the same qualities to the physiology of the body. Then turmoil ceases to exist. In still another reading, Cayce says,

> For, as Life is continuous, then the soul finds itself both in eternity and in spirit; in mind, yet in materiality.
>
> If these become confused by the desires of self-aggrandizement or self-indulgence, or the glory of self for fame, for fortune or any of those that are considered as ideal conditions in a material plane, then the entity becomes confused.

But as has been indicated, if there is the continuous use of spiritual force, spiritual value in relationships to the mental and material, there is harmony, peace, understanding and wisdom in the knowledge of the divinity within. [1353-1]

It is important to recognize that the manifestation of love or warfare throughout all aspects of our mind and its choices is the activity of the soul-self following either its ideal in the Christ Consciousness or else digressing into self-centeredness. Thus, when all these different influences are finally filtered down into the systems and organs of the body, e.g., the life-support systems, they bring either peace, harmony, balance, understanding, and trust—or the opposite, which can be simply described as turmoil.

And turmoil in the functional parts of our bodies will eventually bring us to the experience of what we have come to call, over the ages, a disease or an illness. It is one of God's ways of getting our attention.

CHAPTER 11

Healthful Diet and the Creative Life Force

We all eat, and most of us love it. Not only is it necessary for the continuity of life, but special holidays, like Christmas and Thanksgiving, also provide us with evidence that there is a spiritual aspect to the simple act of sitting down and sharing a meal with others.

The inner search for a deeper meaning in life blossomed in my experience when I recognized that our eating habits and choice of foods were important factors in bringing about healing of the body. And I came to recognize over the years that there needed to be a unified effort between the individual and the Creative Forces of the Universe as healing progressed.

Try as we may, we cannot avoid the presence of the Divine in our relationships, and certainly in the foods that we eat. Developments over recent years offer increasing evidence that foods, well chosen, provide an important foundation for building health in our bodies, no matter what ails us.

One rule in your search, then, in building health through sensible eating habits might be to repeat in your mind over and over again that the Life Force is always at work within your own body, influencing all the functioning parts in an effort to bring about a balance—not only in your body, but also in the relationships that exist between your body, your mind, and your spiritual reality.

As the food performs its function, and the Life Force adds its primary efforts, you need to recall, over and over again, that our lives are built from what we put into our mouths and what we put into our heads, or what we think. Both are important: feeding our bodies and feeding our minds. These are the building blocks that create a strong, healthy temple.

If you are successful in making close contact with the power of the Life Force (through attitudes, through prayer and meditation, or through living the concepts identified with your ideal), then another step in achieving a coordination within the body functions is accomplished, and you have made the move toward health rather than toward illness or a dis-ease.

Remember that the whole body—physically, mentally, spiritually—is one, and that when the individual parts coordinate, even the foods that you've chosen in your particular diet create a better effort within the body to attain a normal balance and activity.

We understand that the Life Force—the God Force—that gives us life and remains active within our beings, is doing the best that it can to create health, despite the blocks we may have built and what we might do unknowingly in opposing that effort. Thus it becomes evident that we need to cooperate with all the food that we take into our bodies, blessing it at the beginning of the meal and visualizing it doing its assigned job while we are eating.

It is also important that we do not bring discord into the environment while eating, for functional changes will occur in the digestive tract, bringing changes in the acid output, in the peristalsis and thus in the assimilation of life-giving forces. So don't argue at mealtime! Allow peace to come to the adrenal glands. Of course, it is best not to fight at any time, if it can be avoided. The earth is a strange place, however, and sometimes discord does come into our experience in ways that do not seem to be preventable. But it is wonderful to strive for harmonious, fun-filled mealtimes. Food should be an occasion for sharing with others not only your thoughts and your presence, but also the warmth of your love and your joy. Enjoy your food and laugh often. "Keep the juices flowing" is a good policy to follow, and an excellent strategy to employ with others.

There are several simple concepts about food found in the Cayce readings. He would talk about how certain foods would affect the function of the pylorus, the stomach, or other parts of the digestive tract, for example, where the acid and enzymes of the stomach and the small bowel go through changes necessary for normal assimilation. He could anticipate problems occurring with improper dietary practices which might not be serious at the time, but could build toward difficulties if continued. He also stressed a need to avoid certain combinations of foods. For instance:

- Citrus and cereals (or milk) are not to be eaten together.
- Avoid milk or cream with your coffee or tea.
- Fruits and vegetables should not be eaten at the same meal.
- Don't eat meat or cheese with starchy foods.
- Don't cook vegetables with meat or meat fats.

The basic Cayce diet would avoid these combinations which are fairly well known in most kitchens today. In the usual meal planning, it was his idea that there would be two or three vegetables grown above the ground and one grown below. He suggested that fish, fowl, or lamb was best for gaining sufficient protein, and that the diet should be slightly alkaline overall. To achieve this alkaline state, he recommended using four alkaline-reacting foods daily to one that is acid-reacting. Red meats, fats, gravies, sugars, and most starches and sweets are acid-reacting, while most vegetables and fruits are of the alkaline-reacting nature. Today we agree that a highly vegetarian diet is best.

But why alkaline? As we stated previously in the discussion on colds, the immune system needs to be on the alkaline side, slightly higher in its pH than the bloodstream, so the elements that protect us—specifically the white blood cells and the gamma globulins—will stay healthy and effective in their process of protecting and rebuilding our bodies.

Locally grown foods are optimal to keep one attuned to the local environment—one good reason to grow food in your own garden. Cayce was also an early teacher and advocate of growing foods organically.

It is also best to drink six to eight glasses of water every day, preferably a glassful before and after each meal, plus enough at other times to fill out your quota. One meal should consist of nothing but a fresh green salad alternated with soup on occasion.

These basic rules are what are being generally endorsed today by dieticians, nutritionists, cardiovascular specialists, and oncologists to prevent heart and vascular disease, as well as cancer. And those who are most advanced in their thinking also see evidence of treatment for these diseases coming from the area of the diet that we eat.

Different cultures—those in the very cold countries, like the land of the eskimos, for instance, and those who live in the equatorial parts of the earth—have different needs in food selections from what we do in the moderate climates. Basically, however, Cayce recommended never overeating or bolting one's food. We need to avoid heavy foods at lunchtime, and generally avoid at all times fats (such as pork), fried foods, white flour, and white sugar. Cayce saw crisp bacon as an exception to the pork part of the menu.

It seems to me remarkable that a man like Cayce, who had relatively little education, could lie down on a couch, go into an altered state of consciousness, and come up with information about health and diet that was decades in advance of present knowledge of prevention and resolution of certain diseases—the use of fibers in the diet, for example, and a low fat regimen to prevent cancers and heart disease. Cayce did this, however, and his suggestions were valid and proven to be helpful as time progressed.

Cayce's specific remarks regarding cancer centered around the diet as a preventative measure, as well as a prescriptive one. He also recommended evaluating and improving emotions and attitudes, since there is always a need for more patience, persistence, and consistency in our efforts to achieve good health. The specifics of his suggestions to a variety of individuals who were afflicted with cancer can be found in those readings, where he saw the functioning of each person's internal workings to be unique for that individual.

But perhaps the real essence of prevention and eventual cure of such a condition as cancer can be found in the following quote:

> For, in each physical organism there are those conditions that enable the organ to reproduce itself, if it has the cooperation of every other portion of the body. When these suffer from mental or physical disorders that make for repressions in any portion of the system, then first dis-ease and distress arise. If heed is not taken as to the warnings sent forth along the nervous systems of the body indicating that certain organs or portions of the system are in distress, or the SOS call that goes out is not heeded, then disease sets in.
>
> What are the disturbing factors, then, in this physical organism?
>
> There has not been the response to those calls for aid in the physical functioning of the body.[531-2]

So where does this take us, in relationship to cancer, from the preventative measures that might be taken, to what might be done after its very earliest stages, to measures to be taken following the most extensive metastases?

My experience, and my knowledge of the Cayce readings, lead me to understand that the very first item that should be tended to is one's spiritual path and relationship to the Divine. Very simply, Jesus said, "Seek ye first the kingdom of God, and his righteousness, and all these things shall be added unto you" (Matt. 6:33). We are spiritual beings, traveling our path toward oneness in this earthly domain. Thus we need to remind ourselves that our origin and our destiny lie in another dimension—we are indeed eternal beings. We are guests here, being given opportunities always to learn how to love one another. And ourselves.

Once that firm foothold is established, then we need to use our own creativity in seeking out all those means available to aid us in the healing process, including our minds and our spirits. It doesn't matter whether it is castor oil packs, a proper diet, or even the surgeon's knife. We need to believe that healing can happen, and then live the experience to make it happen.

A woman whom I'll call Isabelle is a perfect case in point. Diagnosed as having a rectal cancer twenty-five years ago, Isabelle knew the therapy proposed would be an abdominal-perineal resection—the entire rectum and part of the lower colon would be removed and a colostomy would be created on the abdominal wall.

Isabelle, in her mid-fifties and a registered nurse, knew what all this meant—and she didn't want surgery. She was also well informed about the Edgar Cayce material, so she moved to Phoenix temporarily and spent the next year and a half being treated at the A.R.E. Clinic. When the program was completed, her surgeon removed a shrunken bit of tissue on the lining of the rectal wall—all that was left of the cancer.

Isabelle's therapy program included a special diet, therapeutic massages, colonics, violet ray treatments (a transcutaneous electric treatment), counseling, biofeedback training, and regular medical evaluation. Her diet was probably the most remarkable item in her regimen of therapy. It followed one of the Cayce readings which recommended a diet that a cow or a rabbit would eat. This was given for a person who had far advanced cancer, but Isabelle was agreeable to do whatever needed to be done.

She followed such a diet, eating nothing but green salads for nearly nine months, lost twenty pounds during the first couple of months, but then stabilized and maintained a constant weight of about 125 pounds the rest of the time. After the nine months, fruit was gradually added to her diet, and it stayed that way until the surgeon pronounced her cured.

What brought about the healing of such a lesion? The diet, certainly, but also her dreams were encouraging throughout, and her attitudes of constructive beliefs, the various therapies, and the prayers that so many people were sending out into the ethers—all these things contributed to the end product.

To understand a bit of what might have been going on inside Isabelle's body, we would have to look at the physiological processes that were changing and improving. The following reading was given for someone else, of course, because Cayce had been gone for twenty-five years when Isabelle found that she had cancer. But the reading gives us an insight into what might have been going on with Isabelle.

> *But we would make changes in the manner in which the assimilations are carried on, the manner in which the circulations are distributed through the impulses from various ganglia or centers along the cerebrospinal system from which organs of the body may be made to properly coordinate: the organs of the pelvis as well as the hepatic circulation and the activities to the respiratory system.*
>
> *Thus there may be allowed the elimination of drosses, the elimination of energies or used forces that become as drosses in the activity of the system: so that the activity may become nominal or normal.* [1073-1]

Overcoming a cancer is not simply removal of the group of cells that are apparently causing the difficulty. It means correcting the basic cause of the problem—whether it be attitudes, circulation, neurology, acid-alkaline balance, or whatever—and changing the physiology of the body so that it functions constructively, not in a destructive manner that brings death. This is the manner in which Cayce saw the "forces" within the body acting, always related to emotions, stresses, attitudes, and the belief patterns of the unconscious mind. All these factors find their home base in the autonomic nervous system of the body, and in the endocrine glands, and they have the major role in establishing the balance and coordination within the physiology of the body which allows, in turn, for a homeostasis that brings healing. A simplified concept, but certainly significant in the care of the human body.

CHAPTER 12

Healing, Regeneration, and Longevity

"The spirit you're channeling may be your own!" Jerry Kvasnicka minced no words in an article in *Integrity International* (January/February 1988), for he saw no reason why each of us might not be in direct communication with the source of truth. "If you have a valid perception of truth why not give yourself a little credit before leaping to the conclusion that it must have originated with a disembodied entity? . . . Why not replace this counterfeit identity with the genuine article—'made in the image and likeness of God'? Yes, *all* of us!"

Edgar Cayce repeated this kind of information to seekers through most of five decades as he reminded us that we, as souls, are created in the likeness of God and need to start acting in that manner. Our dreams, our feelings, our moments of insight during meditation, even our hunches, are touching that source of all truth.

Healing was the subject of Cayce's discourses more than 65 percent of the time, and he urged us to consult the physician within, the Christ Consciousness. Touching that source, whether through one of the insights that arise in dreams, meditation, or in a hunch entering an extended state of consciousness, as Cayce did, can bring truth to the world and healing to the body.

What most of us forget, however, is that action within our bodies must follow whatever insight that may come to us. Cayce reminded us in reading 257-191 that there is present in each physical body the ability for the body to revive, to resuscitate, and to reorganize itself continuously. He added that the glands of the body produce all the elements for this rejuvenation of normal functioning of the nervous system and the organs of the body. It's our responsibility to add to our diet and exercise programs those things that give the glands the sustenance they need. We need to hold the attitudes that are constructive, develop the emotional patterns that build, and continue the physical care that may be needed.

Let's not be overanxious, then, in rebuilding or creating health for our bodies. Instead, let's search out the truth for ourselves. Let's look at the truth that has come from those in the past who have committed themselves to serve God, and know that simple applications, as well as thoughts, attitudes, emotions, and prayers, can bring healing and balance. It's not simple, but it truly is an adventure in consciousness.

This brings me to the subject of castor oil. God must have had a sense of humor, to cloak such a wonderful healing substance in the smile that often accompanies its mention. But the castor bean plant was called the Palma Christi in the Middle Ages—and I'm sure the person who gave it this honor knew that it was indeed like touching the body with the palm of the Christ.

Castor oil is used daily in our practice at the A.R.E. Clinic. One of my favorite patients several years ago was ninety-three years old. George had a large growth on his right earlobe—a keratosis—which was disfiguring, although not malignant. Some of these skin problems do, however, become cancerous. His had been treated by several other doctors before I saw him, but the keratosis persisted. I instructed him to rub castor oil thoroughly on the earlobe twice daily, and clean it off with a soft cloth. After not seeing him for a year and a half, I checked his ear and found that it was completely normal—no keratosis—but he was still using the castor oil, because, he said, it made his ear feel so soft.

Another patient, Susan, used castor oil packs on her abdomen periodically throughout her pregnancy. In addition, she rubbed castor oil on her abdomen once or twice a day, with the result that she developed no stretch marks, even though her family is prone to this problem, and she herself had some on her hips and breasts during puberty. "I started using castor oil on my face also after noticing early in my pregnancy that I was developing acne. It cleared up and my face stayed so clear that most people mistook me for twenty-three or twenty-four, although I am thirty-five years of age."

Cayce described at least thirty different physiological functions that were changed for the better through the use of castor oil applied topically, mostly by the use of packs. The oil brought results such as increasing eliminations, stimulating liver function, dissolving and removing lesions and adhesions, reducing toxemia, increasing lymphatic circulation, reducing inflammation, increasing relaxation, improving liver and kidney coordination, relieving headaches, and increasing skin circulation.

God created Cayce in His image. Cayce used his talents to help others. You are also created in God's image. You can also contact that source of truth. Perhaps the real lesson when we contact the physician within is that when we do make the contact, our purpose here on earth is to use that information to aid in the healing of our own bodies and then help those whom we meet, day by day, in whatever way we can, recognizing that we do the most through manifesting the nature of the Divine, which is spelled very simply as L-O-V-E.

When I began using the Cayce remedies rather extensively, and later applied basic Cayce concepts to the process of healing, my correspondence and telephone conversations with A.R.E. members began proliferating, with stories of how the body responds to its divine nature as it fashions a wholeness out of what was formerly distress and disease. For example, I received a card several

Christmases ago picturing a beautiful little three-year-old girl, Lily, in her new red dress, sitting on one of those big, soft, stuffed animals. She was smiling from ear to ear, and you couldn't ask for a lovelier girl.

Her mother wrote what was a tribute to Cayce, for one of his life desires was to help children. She said: "I wrote to you and we talked on the phone nearly two and a half years ago.

"Our daughter was born with pulmonary atresia with hypoplastic right ventricle. [That means Lily was born with congenital closure of the pulmonary valve between the right ventricle and the pulmonary artery. Her right ventricle was also hypoplastic, which means that it was defective in its development, undoubtedly smaller than normal.] You suggested castor oil packs, which I did, and much prayer, which we did and still do. She also took Chinese herbs and was able to have corrective surgery. Well, look at her now! Thank God and may God bless Edgar Cayce."

The healing of the body meant development of more normal functions. This allowed the healing of surgery to be accomplished. Now Lily has a chance to live out a very normal life.

The entire procedure reminds me of what Edgar Cayce said in so many ways—that healing can come from the laying on of hands, from prayer, physical therapy, or even the knife. It all hinges on what is happening inside the individual. Is there an awakening of the spiritual nature of the one being healed? With Lily, how could there not be that awakening, with her parents loving her as they obviously do and praying for her?

The little girl's mother exercised faith in God, applied patience, persistence, and consistency, along with the castor oil packs, and the results were obvious. Cayce talked about healing in so many ways. In one reading, he told an enquiring woman (not Lily's mother):

For all healing must come from that within that is of a spiritual import. Leave the results with the Giver of all good and perfect gifts. Be consistent

and persistent in thy physical and thy spiritual and thy mental reactions
for the better result. For the laws of the Lord are perfect, converting the
soul. [1199-2]

In his sleeping state, Cayce saw illness in the human being as
the end point of malfunctioning physiology. Thus, in an attempt
to correct the ailing body, the suggestions were aimed at the functioning parts—the physiology—not at the end point of a process.
This is a very important distinction, for it points out the difference between the manner in which Cayce looked at this individual created in the image of God, and the manner in which I was
taught to search for a diagnosis and, in a sense, not look at the
human being whose physiology created the problem in the first
place.

Healing, regeneration, and longevity are all interrelated and
could be considered as identical. If one brings about true healing to a body, this creates regeneration. And if different portions
of the body are regenerated—and coordinated with the rest of
the body—that individual is not likely to die as soon as he
would have otherwise. This, of course, is one example of
longevity.

Methuselah, according to biblical accounts, lived longer than
any other individual. He was 969 years old when he died in the
great flood. I have often wondered why he and other patriarchs of
biblical history lived so long and today we really stretch it to live
into our eighties.

There are those, however, in modern times who have made it
well over the century mark. In the late 1960s several physicians
and researchers brought a man from Colombia, South America, to
New York, where they performed multiple evaluations of his
physiological status. He was known to be 150 years old, but his
smile, his attitudes, and his ability to read without glasses led one
to believe he was perhaps in his sixties or seventies. His blood
pressure, cardiogram, body weight, and pulse were all normal. In
short, he was healthy. He enjoyed New York food, but was soon

taken back home. He thought at that time that he was the oldest man in the world.

I've told the story often of a woman, who lived on the shores of the Black Sea, and who appeared on educational TV. A team of reporters was sent to do a documentary on her birthday party. She was to be 145, and the party was held outside one of her homes, at a long table where there were perhaps fifteen or twenty participants seated. All at the table were a hundred years old or older. One was the birthday woman's son, who was 109. The younger people in the crowd surrounding the table had to stand—including the 90-year-olds. The celebrants at the table were mostly all drinking vodka and smoking up a storm.

I was struck with the incongruity of the picture—centenarians manifesting the ability to live over a hundred years, yet smoking and drinking, which we believe to cause illness and shorten one's life span. In trying to reconcile these apparent opposites, I thought of George Burns smoking a cigar. Then I remembered that Jesus told us that it was more important what comes out of your mouth than what goes in. I would suppose this means alcohol or smoking. But the consciousness has to be considered, and we know that we build with our minds what we really, deep down, want to build. Even as far as our own health and longevity are considered.

Perhaps the most fascinating story of longevity is found in a set of books written in the early years of this century by Baird T. Spalding (*Life and Teaching of the Masters of the Far East*), who, with ten of his fellow researchers, visited the Far East in 1894. They contacted the Great Masters of the Himalayas. It took a while before they found out that these apparently young men were indeed hundreds of years old. Some had lived two thousand years. As they grew in spiritual awareness, they apparently had learned the laws that permit the regeneration of the body. Their purpose, apparently, was to aid the world in various ways to make for a more harmonious and loving environment throughout the earth.

They were able to bilocate, to materialize food out of the air. They supplied everything needed for their daily wants directly from the Universal, including food, clothing, and money. When occasion required, they would walk on water, go through fire, travel in the invisible, and do many other things that we have been accustomed to look upon as miraculous, performed only by those possessed of supernatural powers.

The travelers watched while one of these individuals parted two jackals that were fighting over the body of a smaller animal they had killed. When he approached them, the jackals stopped fighting and put their heads in his outstretched hands in perfect trust, then resumed their meal in quiet. He then spoke to Spalding and said, "This is not the mortal self, the self you see, that is able to do these things. It is a truer, deeper self. It is what you know as God, God within me, God the Omnipotent One working through me, that does these things. Of myself, the mortal self, I can do nothing. It is only when I get rid of the outer entirely and let the actual, the I AM, speak and work and let the great Love of God come forth that I can do these things that you have seen. When you let the love of God pour through you to all things, nothing fears you and no harm can befall you."

In John (14:10–12), Jesus said, "Anyone who has seen me has seen the Father. Then how can you say, 'Show us the Father'? Do you not believe that I am the Father and the Father is me? I am not myself the source of the words I speak to you: it is the Father who dwells in me doing his own work. Believe me when I say that I am in the Father and the Father is me; or else accept the evidence of the deeds themselves. In truth, in very truth I tell you, he who has faith in me will do what I am doing; and he will do greater things still because I am going to the Father."

In my search of the Cayce readings on longevity, I found one woman who was told, concerning her projected life span, that "one can make that [life span] almost what one wishes!" (338-5). One of the readings admonished "Keep the pineal gland operating and you won't grow old—you will always be young" (294-141). And Cayce pointed to the Peyer's Patches in the small bowel as being an important part of producing longevity in the human being.

The important question here is "How does one keep the pineal gland operating?" Here are a few nuggets of truth which I found.

Cayce describes a relationship between the pineal and the Leydig cells, located respectively in the testes in the male and the ovaries in the female. The pineal is described in the reading as the builder very early on in the development of the fetus, in utero. It becomes the brain in the development of the fetus, communicating with the brains or consciousnesses of the parents of the child. Then, as the child is born and the cord is cut, it takes on the ability to imagine, and becomes closely related to the sensory mechanisms, the cerebrospinal nervous system, and the autonomic.

In the Cayce description of the pineal, there is found a distinct relationship between the sexual functions and the pineal. And, as various stages of the qualities that we know as love (patience, kindness, brotherly love) are manifested throughout, the pineal gland continues operating.

How, then, to bring about longevity through this gland and its workings? We need certainly to take care of our bodies in many ways, but need—above all—simply to apply love in our lives.

The rules of longevity are not complicated, but are indeed difficult for most of us to follow. We need to take seriously the application of patience, persistence, and consistency in all therapy procedures that are begun, whether it be exercise, diet, use of herbs, castor oil packs, or whatever. These qualities are part of what can be understood as the manifestation of love. It's that word again, over and above all the individual treatment modalities one might undertake.

And Cayce's information also promises the possibility of healing of every nature, insisting in the strongest terms that no condition of physical illness would remain if the treatment procedure were taken patiently, consistently, and persistently in any body.

If our nature is genuinely spiritual, and we are here on the earth to learn those lessons that give us forward movement on the path back to our source, then the important thing is to learn from every experience something that helps us to fulfill our purpose for entering the earth plane.

The purpose, then, is to experience soul growth, rather than simply to stick around here a long time. If long life helps you to learn more (and this is very important!), then make your journey this time around a long one and full of joy and wonderful experiences—but especially make them learning experiences.

A well-documented study was conducted by Georgi A. Pitskhelauri on longevity among men and women in Soviet Georgia. Published in the United States in 1982, *The Longliving of Soviet Georgia* reports on these older people, their lifestyles, their habits, and their diets. Dr. Pitskhelauri found that their eating habits, for instance, were very simple—meat was used very infrequently, and some were lacto-vegetarians. One of the outstanding findings was that these people were nearly always peasants or those who had spent most if not all of their lives on the farm, and they worked—most of them—till they finally dropped.

One man worked until he was 144 years old. His brother died when he was 149. Perhaps the best known, and one of the oldest, of those investigated, was Shirali Mislimov, from Soviet Azerbaijan. I followed his career for several years, and read where, at the age of 167, he was still caring for his orchard and riding his horse. He became internationally famous because of his age. He finally died at 169, having been a sheepherder most of his life. Many challenged the statistics of his birthdate, and so on, but Soviet officials pointed to their Social Security type of records to substantiate his age.

Pitskhelauri recounts how the classification and nomenclature of elderly or old people came about. It was accepted first in Leningrad in June of 1962, then passed by the World Health Organization in Kiev in May of 1963. Table 3 will tell you when you will start maturing, if you have not already reached that level.

Class	Nomenclature
60–74 years	Mature
75–89 years	Old
90 plus	Longliving

TABLE 3. PITSKHELAURI'S CLASSIFICATION OF ELDERLY.

Contigern (San Mungo), the founder of the bishopric of Glasgow, and Ktsarten Petrark both lived to be 185. Other historical examples of longevity include Thomas Parr, who was presented to the king in London at the age of 152 as an example of longevity, and R. Taylor, a postal clerk who received a gift from Queen Victoria in honor of his great age. He was so excited about the gift that he died three months later, at 134 years of age.

The oldest of the longliving recorded in Pitskhelauri's book was an Iranian, Saied Abutalim Musavi, who lived in a little village 550 miles south of Tehran. He was 191 at the time the doctor finished writing his book.

The most consistent and valuable lifestyle contribution to length of life reported by those who have done the living is simply their work. They all kept at it until they were ready to leave. In the United States, it's called "dying with your boots on!"

In our part of the world, no similar study has yet been done, to my knowledge. Some years ago, a "Normative Aging Study" was published by the Veterans Administration which forecast a normal life expectancy of 120 to 140 years for the average American, if he were to utilize all the knowledge about care of the human body that is currently available. About the same time this was published in 1973, a newspaper story appeared about Charlie Smith, who lived in Bartow, Florida, and who was celebrating his 131st birthday as the oldest man in the United States drawing Social Security payments. Charlie finally died at 139, and his 79-year-old son attended his funeral.

A psychotherapist who has been an A.R.E. member for a number of years sent me a series of dreams that had to do with his desire to regenerate the midline area of his abdomen. It seems he had developed an abdominal hernia which his surgeon wanted to repair with the lowering of the knife in the surgical amphitheater. Our friend did not want that to happen.

He dreamed about a beautiful wooden boat in a dry dock large enough for bays—but not the ocean. "The midline on the bottom looks a little off but the shape of the boat is perfect. There are two pieces of wood running down the middle of the boat that have been stained." There was more to the dream, but he felt that his body was the boat; the two pieces of wood were his rectus abdomini muscles. And after he started using a massage oil on his abdomen (containing tincture of myrrh), he was intrigued to notice that this particular oil looked much like the wood stain.

The dreamer obviously felt that the dream guidance he received was intended to tell him that he indeed could regenerate that portion of his body that had become weakened, and that surgery was not the only manner of healing. He had come in contact with some of the Cayce readings about this subject, perhaps even the two that follow:

For as the body is the storehouse of all influences and forces from without, it has the abilities for the creating—with the correct firing or fuel for the body—that which is able to sustain, not only sustain but to recuperate and to rebuild, revitalize, regenerate the activities of the body. [1334-1]

For, as the body is an atomic structure . . . as these atoms, as these structural forces are made to conform or to rely upon or to be one with the spiritual import, the spiritual activity, they revivify, they make for constructive forces.

The soul cannot die; for it is of God. The body may be revivified, rejuvenated. And it is to that end it may, the body, transcend the Earth and its influence. [262-85]

Cayce let those who were present at the reading know that they were not among the select who might at that time "transcend the Earth." Comforting thought! In any event, it becomes obvious that the essence of the Cayce material is that we are eternal beings, spiritual in nature, and with powers within that have only occasionally been tapped.

Scientists have been at work on the same subject, but for the most part approaching it from a different point of view. Robert O. Becker, an orthopedic research surgeon, pioneered work on regeneration some three decades ago. He observed the ability of the salamander to regenerate a leg when it was amputated, and he postulated that the frog—which does not normally regrow limbs—could do this also, if the key to regeneration could be found. He found it in low-voltage electricity which he measured in the salamander after amputation, and then replicated in the frog. And the frog regrew its leg after amputation.

Researchers from the University of California at San Diego and La Jolla Cancer Research Center have brought about brain cell regeneration in rats. These scientists took strips of tissue from human placenta and implanted them in rat brains in which two sections of the brain—the hippocampus and the septum—had been disconnected. The implant stimulated growth of nerve cells across the "bridge" to reconnect them. The researchers feel that when and if this is able to be utilized in humans, it will be most helpful in spinal cord injuries.

Rockefeller Institute scientists have discovered that the aging brains of canaries routinely grow new neurons. Anatomists at the University of Rochester have regrown severed neurons in the brains of aged rats. Stanford researchers have discovered in rats a protein that seems to promote the regrowth of damaged nerves. Such protein, however, while increasing in amount after a nerve injury, accumulates only in the peripheral nerves, not in the central nervous system. Other researchers have used a silicon tube as a tunnel through which nerve tissue has grown in the rat. Still others have grafted peripheral nerve tissue to the two ends of a rat's severed optic nerve, which then grew back, and apparently functioned normally.

Still others, such as David Hedley Wilson of Leeds University in England, used pulsed high-frequency electromagnetic energy to treat paralysis and bring about functional, and apparently structural, regeneration of afflicted nerves. Then Lawrence Kromer at the University of Vermont hypothesized that one reason severed neurons in the central nervous system usually do not regenerate is that scarring prevents it—and his work with brain transplants supported such a concept.

At the A.R.E. Clinic, we cared for a child severely afflicted with Down's syndrome. Many of the therapies found in the Cayce readings were used for more than three years. These included manipulation, loving care, electromagnetic field therapy, castor oil packs, and diet. The boy grew and flourished, was a joy to all, and lost many of the physical findings associated with Down's—even his face became less and less typical of that syndrome.

He had surgery for an associated heart defect. Afterward he never regained the momentum that he had earlier. He died at age five. The autopsy revealed a normal brain, which probably explains why the body had improved so much in spite of the Down's syndrome; Harvey Grady quoted the autopsy report on the brain in the *Journal of Holistic Medicine*: "The cerebral hemisphere appears well developed. There is no obvious gyral anomaly. The configuration and shape of the brain appears within normal limits. There is no obvious flattening of the occipital area as described in Down's syndrome. Likewise, the superior temporal gyrus is not distinctly abnormal. The cerebellum is of its natural size, and normal relation to the brain."

While there could have been no pathological examination of the brain at an early age, the report at the end of this incarnation for the boy showed that regeneration of brain tissue did in reality come about, which helps us to understand that regeneration can come about in any part of the human body.

When one's body begins to "age" or deteriorate, it is a sign that it is in need of healing. True healing will bring with it regeneration, and regeneration means rejuvenation, or the making of the body young once again.

Spalding's books and Cayce's suggestions would lead us to believe that there are those individuals on the earth who have been here for two thousand years or more. To my knowledge I have not met any of these people, but I suspect that if they knew enough about regeneration to keep the body healthy and active all those years, it would be difficult to tell just how old they might be. When your hair is neither gray nor absent, and when your face is not really wrinkled and your step is young, how old would you look? It was said of Moses that when he was ready to die at 120, his eyes were clear and his natural forces unabated.

Pathologists never diagnose death as being caused by old age when they do an autopsy. They find disease, deterioration, or accident as the cause of death. In a very real sense, it's difficult to die any other way—and we must all take leave of the earth one way or another.

Cayce's position was that we are all eternal beings, and we can spend whatever time we need in order to fulfill our purpose in the earth this incarnation. I've wondered, too, if it isn't possible to fulfill that purpose we chose for a given lifetime, then decide to choose another purpose before giving up the earth life this time around. If we feel so well that there is no benefit in leaving, just to come around again as a little child, it seems reasonable to consider this as a possibility. It would, however, require application along the lines of the concepts found in the following two readings.

> *All healing of every nature is the changing of the vibrations from within—the attuning of the Divine within the living tissue of a body to Creative Energies. Whether it is accomplished by the use of drugs, the knife or whatnot, it is the attuning of the atomic structure of the living cellular force to its spiritual heritage.* [1967-1]

For there is every infusion within a normal body to replenish itself. And if
there will be gained that consciousness, there need not be ever the necessity
of a physical organism aging—other than that as is the nominal desire of a
body to give away to the surrounding forces or for its own rest. [1299-1]

If we are to give way to the surrounding forces, we are probably allowing ourselves to be adversely influenced by the stresses
that are part of every life—and that will indeed age us. If I were
to desire that kind of respite that Cayce discussed, it would probably mean that I was tired of this experience on the earth and
wanted to leave. In the Bible, Paul longed for the heavenly home,
as some call it, and he probably knew something about what it
was like.

Since we are eternal, anyway, there is a time for us to come to
the earth and a time to leave. It seems that birth into this dimension is quite like birth into the life that we call spiritual. Both of
them involve death but both bring us into a new realm of learning how to experience—and manifest—the joy, the gentleness, the
forgiveness and understanding that are part of the Life Force
which we call Love, or God.

What brings about long life such as Shirali had in Russia and
Charlie Smith experienced here in our own country? I'm sure it is
part of the total picture of healing of the body, for over and over
again, every seven years, each of these individuals replaced every
single atom in his body—just as you and I do. Many aspects of
their lives had to be harmonious, for discord did not destroy
them. Their outlook was for peace and for making themselves of
service in some way to their fellow man.

Our seeking to be of service may simply be the manifestation
of a purpose which we chose before being born. For we each have
a purpose, although it may lie deep within ourselves and never be
consciously recognized. Cayce suggested that we keep fit for a
purpose. That would likely bring about longevity in itself, but he
had more to say about that purpose:

the purpose for which each entity—yea, this entity—enters the material ex-
perience; that the glory of the Lord, as manifested in the entity itself, may
be magnified in the earth. [3459-1]

Looking at the larger picture, one would see Charlie or one of
these other long-living persons moving into a new experience in
the spiritual realm for whatever purpose meets the needs of the
soul—and then reentering this dimension once again as a little
child, undoubtedly with the built-in certainty that long life is as
natural as being born.

PART THREE

The Spirit

CHAPTER 13

The Soul's Journey

For, as the entity finds, we are body, we are mind, we are soul. The soul is in the image of God, thus eternal, everlasting. Life in its expression, then, in a mental and in a material world, is only a mental and material manifestation of the soul-entity; that which was brought into being as a part of Creative Forces. Thus it is eternal. 3459-1

Throughout the Cayce readings, the theme is repeated over and over again—as in a symphony—that all life has a purpose and each individual at the soul level strives to find that purpose for being in this incarnation. It has something very vital to do with the process of being healed, for again and again the readings questioned those seeking healing of the physical body: "What do you want to be healed *for*? What is your life's purpose?"

When we think of ourselves as a continuing stream of consciousness, we start to think in terms of repeated lives on the earth. Then we ask ourselves, Where did we come from? What really is our origin? After that, we begin to wonder in terms of Where are we going? That gets a little heavy, until we gain some basic beliefs about life itself that we can accept.

We really have our beginnings in a spiritual dimension, don't we? God created us in His image—spiritual beings, like Him. And our direction is toward that source where we had our beginning. It is those periods in the earth between the start and the finish of a particular adventure that give us the difficulties. We call those "life." And in this third dimension, we find life is an encounter with a multitude of individuals, and sometimes a multifaceted situation called dis-ease or disease, illness, sickness, or feeling bad. Whatever we wish to call it, the situation puts us into a state where we are not experiencing health. To regain health requires an adventure in consciousness.

A young fellow wrote me a letter. He apparently was unsuccessful in his material life, and he felt that he had failed in many ways and described a degree of depression. I reminded him (because he had read the material) that Cayce pointed out to all of us that every experience, whether it is so-called bad or good, is an opportunity for soul growth.

This wasn't to help his feeling of failure, particularly, but what every individual needs to understand—and really *wants* to know—is that the earth plane and our experiences here are not to make us successful in material things but rather to give us opportunities for living the Christ life. Since we were created in the image of God, it is our destiny to return to oneness with Him. That means we are all spiritual beings living in a material world, and we are trying to find the path that leads us back home. And it is important to realize that every illness is a step along the path, if we approach it creatively.

I asked a minister once what happens when we die. He told me that the soul moves on, but his thought was that he was the body, and he, the body, remains in the grave. His problem was that his life had always been oriented around the material world. He had great difficulty in conceiving that he was a spiritual being, like God, just visiting the earth. The gift that Edgar Cayce passed on to us is the clarity of his vision in looking at what the Bible says. We indeed are created in the image of God, as eternal beings who were here before the earth and the solar system even came into

being. There is no death, and true health is found in the consciousness of the oneness we have with that Creative Source.

Sometimes we forget our nature. And thus at times we fail to
realize how deep an impact we can make on the destiny of the
earth and its inhabitants, simply because of what we are. We are
all destined for greater things than we dare imagine. It's time for
us to accept who we are and start taking responsibility for our destiny.

If you look at Diagram 1 once again, it will remind you that
symbolically, and in the essence of things, God and his creatures
are of the same substance, the difference being that we, as His
children, have not yet learned how infinite and all-absorbing the
quality of love is, and that God is truly love. We are in the process
of learning about it. Thus here we are in the earth. God exercised
the power of choice in creating us in His image. We have exercised
our own gift of choice in choosing to come into the earth—and,
in the process, of course, choosing our parents—to find out what
wonderful kinds of experiences we will be encountering. It truly
is an adventure.

When we came into the earth environs this lifetime, we
changed from our original spiritual form to a configuration that
drew from the elements of the earth and was best suited to be active in this world of ours. Our physical body accommodates more
information and patterns than we can readily imagine. We call this
world a three-dimensional reality, but that has yet to be proved,
for its substance is energy in the form of atoms. It's not really understood, for we say we are in a universe that encompasses many
solar systems and galaxies, yet we cannot understand where this
or other universes end—and we cannot conceive of how it can
end. What is on the other side of the end of all those universes?
We don't know! Our conception of this universe is sometimes
shattered by what we call reality.

We brought with us a history, however, of experiences in living
through a multitude of incarnations in the earth—and also perhaps in other solar systems. But for the present time, it is enough

of a revolution in thought to handle just this earth system and our experiences through many of those lifetimes lost in the distant eons of time. But we do need to look at what we have given ourselves in the way of a heritage. And do it from a perspective that takes into consideration what we truly are—our being, our origin, and our destiny.

During these lifetimes we spend here in the earth, we gain here and there, and sometimes lose ground. But always we are searching for that prize that we sometimes don't even know exists, for our memory at birth is usually clouded.

Many of us in the United States don't even believe that we were in existence before we were born and do not buy into the concept of reincarnation, in spite of the validity given it throughout most of the world cultures. The Cayce readings deal with it constantly and point out the need for it in making sense of our lives as a whole.

Rabbi Herbert Weiner is an authority on the Kabala, the Jewish book of wisdom based on an esoteric interpretation of the Hebrew scriptures. His account to me of how we come into the world helped me to understand more clearly the nature of the realm where we were created—mostly because it recognizes the existence we all had before we were born. But it also speaks of angels, which are part of the text of the Old and the New Testament.

The story he told me was about the Angel of Forgetfulness. It seems that before we are born, we are taken to see what is going to happen in the life planned for us. The angel places a light on our forehead, it shines forward like a movie, and we see all that is to become part of this next lifetime.

Usually one has a choice as to where one is going to be born, so we can exercise choice of location. But when we choose a family, and a group of experiences, the angel touches us on the upper lip and we forget everything we saw. Then we are born.

Perhaps, however, we don't completely forget everything we saw, or some of our prior experiences in the earth. So memory does occasionally persist from times past, whether it be this or another lifetime. And it gives glimpses of past experiences and insights into the nature of the soul that has been doing this traveling through time and space.

In reality, then, there is no death, only the transition between the two dimensions with which we are currently dealing, for we are born into the spiritual dimension when we die to this earth life. And, likewise, we die to the spiritual environment when we arrive again here, on the birth scene with a new set of parents. Cayce touched often on this subject:

> *For, as the entity finds, we are body, we are mind, we are soul. The soul is in the image of God, thus eternal, everlasting Life in its expression, then, in a mental and in a material world, is only a mental and material manifestation of the soul-entity; that which was brought into being as a part of Creative Forces. Thus it is eternal.* 3459-1

> *For it is not all of life to live, nor all of death to die; for one is the beginning of the other, and in the midst of life one is in the midst of death.* 3459-1

> *The passing in, the passing out, is as but the summer, the fall, the spring; the birth into the interim, the birth into the material.* 281-16

Each incarnation in the earth, of course, starts with a choice made as to where and to whom we are going to be born. So our birth each time around takes us into a body-mind-soul complex that satisfies our need to be active in this dimension. We can maintain life through our life-support systems; we can be fully aware through our senses of where we are at any given time; and we can act and be creative in the earth through the nervous system control of our muscles and structural body. So we are prepared to meet what, at the soul level, we need to meet, when we are born to those two people who thus become our parents.

In starting a lifetime, we nearly always lack a conscious memory of any existence prior to birth, although a psychic friend of mine claims that he wants to find a better way of getting into the earth plane than through the channel of birth. It seems that when he was just an infant, he could not stand having women make over him with baby talk, when he knew what they were thinking, and also knew that he was a soul entity who had lived before. But most of us do not remember. So we become programmed to a great extent for this lifetime by the parents and the environment in which we find ourselves. Many of the challenges that come about were, of course, chosen before birth, but the origins of the challenge become lost in the mists of time, in a sense, as the child grows and begins to mature.

His unconscious self, however, brings to conscious view memories from the past, arising as feelings and hunches, some disturbing, some not. Dreams come to the conscious mind, skipping the barrier that usually separates the conscious from the unconscious mind, and thus are born into the child's relationships the turmoils, disturbances, and frustrations that arise from the different paths taken in past lifetimes.

One of the common concepts found in the Cayce readings is that individuals, and sometimes groups, are drawn together because of unfinished business from one lifetime to another. Sometimes mothers have daughters who were mothers to them in a past experience. Or sometimes, lovers in one incarnation become brother and sister in another. It sometimes stretches our beliefs when we look at someone we love deeply this time around and realize that we were perhaps father and son in another encounter. Or sisters. Or enemies who fought each other with sword and spear to the death. We find ourselves to be strange bedfellows in many ways. But it makes sense if we realize we are here to find out how to become more godlike, more active in our daily lives in the manner that God would have us be.

In our residential programs, participants come to know one another at a deep level—sharing life stories in a group setting, eating all their meals together—and often recall, during some of their other therapy sessions, how they might have been together in earlier times in the earth.

One group of nine women—according to their dreams, insights, and visions—had been together as Catholic sisters in a convent in Spain, where they had taken the vow of silence. Mealtimes with this particular group was an experience in itself. At first I thought they were angry with me and wouldn't speak. But they just didn't feel much like talking during the meals. None of them had ever acted like that in their homes, but when brought together, they tuned in to that past incarnation and became Catholic sisters once again. They shared their past experiences with one another—some being dreams, which we discuss at breakfast time, and some being insights in meditation or in group therapy or guided imagery sessions.

One of my past incarnations surfaced when I met the person who had been a monk with me in the church in Rome fifteen hundred years ago. This inclination to be a monk may have moved me years ago to start my college work as a preministerial student.

Most of us who have been working with the ideas and ideals found in the Edgar Cayce readings wonder about past lives— future lives, too, for that matter—and tend to believe that we have been involved in those past experiences one way or another. But it is difficult to comprehend why we, as souls, come back into this environment time and again. What is it we have to learn?

In our Temple Beautiful program, I emphasize to all those who take part that they are indeed eternal beings—and they have a purpose here on the earth plane every time they are born. It may mean that there are bits and pieces of past experiences to set at rest, but primarily they have come back so that they might learn how to love. It seems to be just about that simple. It's what Jesus said—"Love God and love your fellow man!" That's all there is to it.

But how do we understand the transition into the earth plane and then the step back into the spirit after a period of years?

You will notice in Diagram 6 the symbol of body/mind/spirit or soul in the lower left part of the example. The space above the

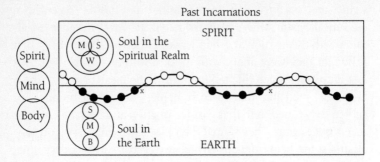

DIAGRAM 6. ENERGIES FROM THE PAST.

horizontal dividing line is termed spirit, while the lower space is given the name of earth plane. The movement on its journey shows the soul acquiring the X (the physical body) on entering the physical plane, and then letting go of it each time it departs for the spiritual realm. So the body stays here, while the soul continues its eternal journey in the spiritual realms, probably preparing for the next visit to the earth.

No matter where we are born, when or to whom, we certainly arrive, and probably choose the parents who are right. So it is we are born again, and again, and again, to keep on learning, and in one manner or another finding ways of healing our bodies, while something very unique and wonderful happens to the soul. Cayce saw each soul, while here on the earth, to be on a path where each experience, if understood, provides a bit of gold, a pearl of great price. And each prize concerns one's destiny in the overall picture:

> *An experience through the earth's plane is for the development of the soul and not mere chance, for there are rules and laws that govern same. And the applications of the spiritual laws are just as definite and MORE true and more sure than those of material orders or material experiences of a material life.*

For as in the material or secular world or rule there are those causes and effects, there are then PRINCIPLES; or an ideal as from which ALL such are judged. And so in the spiritual, in the mental, there are ideals. And these are constructive, and they be founded in those things that are as promises in the experience of man; which begins with "If ye will be my people, I will be thy God—As the man in his experience soweth, so shall he reap—I have made thee a little lower than the angels, that ye might be through thy choice, through thy activity, not only purged from evil influence, evil thought, questionable conditions or experiences, but that ye might be one with me, that ye might know that glory that ye had WITH me before the worlds were."

And thus do those influences come in the experiences of each soul. 1217-1

And here it is again, the promise that recurs throughout the Cayce readings that we are destined to find that awareness that we had with the Creative Forces of the Universe before the worlds came into being. No wonder it is difficult to find that pearl hiding in the midst of each experience. Our destiny is difficult to accept. We've probably proved that by the number of times we have come back into the earth to take the same path once again.

Another Cayce reading gives us some clues in our search to stay on that path:

In thy searching, then, begin with reading each day just a few verses of the 14th, 15th, 16th, and 17th of St. John. First read in the 14th, "In my father's house are many mansions." Dwell on that, not for an hour or a minute but for a day—as ye go about your work. Who is your father? Whom does He mean, in speaking to thee? And what does He mean by mansions? And that there are many mansions in His house? What house? It is indeed thy body, that is the temple. Many mansions are in that body, many temples. For the body has been again and again in the experiences of the earth, and thus they are sometimes mansions, sometimes huts, sometimes homes, and again they become those places where we dislike to abide. 3578-1

Choice is the most precious gift God gave to each of us. Study and application are the key words after choices have been made, but we must first recognize what is to be studied and how to apply it. It does involve our belief patterns, doesn't it? We can choose to believe what we want to believe, in the same manner we can choose our attitudes and emotions. And in a strange manner, these have all been implanted and grow stronger with use in our unconscious mind. They tend to make us feel as if "This is really me," although they have in the past—as well as in the present—only designed the mansion we occupy. And they can be changed. All have a part in the shaping of what we are, whether it is accompanied by illness or abundant health. All those choices we have made have fashioned our bodies to be the temple of the Living God.

But the experiences gained in each incarnation can lead the individual even farther along the chosen path, if the choices taken are of a service that speaks of infinite and creative value to mankind as a whole.

Sometimes, qualities developed in a past life, such as persistence, patience (both constructive in nature), and even hardheadedness (for the most part destructive) can be of benefit in this life. The key is one's direction—is it toward the light or away from it? This is one of the reasons, I believe, that Cayce repeatedly advised those who sought his help that they should choose an ideal, spiritually, mentally, and physically. It is a necessity for every soul who seeks growth.

How do you choose an ideal? It's like the North Star in the sky, something you check with every now and then to be sure you are heading in the right direction. So you might look at your beliefs. Do you believe in God, for instance? Do you choose those things in your life that are creative and constructive? Do you want thoughts that are helpful, kind, and gentle? Do you want to do those things that are beneficial to others? To choose an ideal involves all those aspects of life. The choice always moves one toward the light or away from it—you must make the choice. If we are indeed spiritual beings, then our need is to take as an ideal the direction that moves us toward our destiny. And then we must continually measure our physical, mental, and spiritual lives against the ideal we have chosen. Naturally, as we strive to do that, our ideals will gradually grow clearer and more in line with what we know instinctively inside ourselves is our true nature.

Edgar Cayce talked about reincarnation as the way the soul moves toward becoming a co-creator with God. Having established that as a fact, or at least the perspective taken in the readings, Cayce then went on to make suggestions for the individual looking to him for help. A dominant attitude taken throughout these psychic discourses was to magnify the virtues and minimize the faults. Thus, in discussing past lives, Cayce usually chose incarnations for the questioner where those qualities were built— through the individual's life activities—to benefit mankind, rather than those periods where the soul lost ground. He routinely encouraged people to move always toward the light, toward a greater oneness with the Creative Forces.

He gave such a life reading for a baby boy that not only told of past lives, but also gave advice as to what the parents should do in training and teaching to help this infant grow into adulthood, bringing to flower the promise of giving to the world much in the way of light, love, and music.

Cayce described two of this child's former incarnations. One was where he was a chief musician in the preparation and setting up of the music in the temples for the psalms that were to be sung, and for the Songs of Solomon. In the process, he was associated with David in the planning of the temple in Jerusalem and Solomon afterward when the temple was built.

In another earlier incarnation, in the times of the Temple of Sacrifice and the Temple Beautiful, he was among those who first set the chants of the various peoples to any form of music, and helped to establish chants as part of the activities in the Temple of Sacrifice, and especially as the chants were used in the healing of those that came to the Temple Beautiful.

There were cautions given the parents, however, and instructions about how important it is to help another individual on the path which unfolds the future out of the promise of the past.

Thus we find again the music added to the abilities as a healer, the ability as one to direct . . .

First, to be sure, the developing years have much to do with the choices and the direction the entity may take in giving material expressions of the abilities innate and manifested as the body-mind develops.

Music, as it has been well said, is that expression that spans the distance between the sublime and the ridiculous, that which appeals to the physical, the spiritual, the mental emotions of individuals.

Then, whatever field of direction the entity may take depends much upon whether those emotions are awakened or aroused for the gratifying of material desires, or whether there is the spanning of that realm between the material and the sublime.

These should be kept in that direction, then, in which there may be a completion of that the entity has so oft set in motion in the affairs of men through the experiences or sojourns of the entity in the earth. 2584-1

There are undoubtedly emotions and goals and purposes within each of us that need to be awakened and brought to fruition. It is difficult to move through the early years of any lifetime and come out of it with a clear picture of what was set as the goal or goals at a soul level before taking on the challenge and allowing oneself to be born to those who are capable of helping. But it *can* be done. It just takes dedication by the parents and commitment by the entity who is seeking.

If we put credence in the nearly fifteen thousand readings Cayce gave, then there has been—and may still be—among us this individual, who has made the choices he felt he had to make, and who went through those childhood and teenage years, and is at midlife now. We wonder—has he used music to span the gulf between the sublime and the ridiculous?

If we were to open our own hearts, how would we answer the question about ourselves? Have we taken the high road or the low road? Are our lives now directed toward the Light, toward fulfillment of those activities we never quite finished in past lives and need to complete for the help they may bring to others? These are always questions that we can ask ourselves.

Not only is it a soul search, but it is a factor that needs attention always whenever we find ourselves becoming ill. For our past stays alive within us and we can make it what we will in the present, if we exercise our power to choose. Study Diagram 6. As we pay attention to what has happened in our present life, we may gather—just from a deep insightful contemplation or meditation—information from the past that could be helpful in our healing process or simply in turning our lives around and opening up some wonderful vistas for the future.

Sometimes we forget our soul's eternal nature. Sometimes we fail to realize how deep an impact one man or woman *can* make in the destiny of the earth and its inhabitants. For we are all alike and we are all destined for greater things than we dare imagine. It's time we realize what we are and start acting like it. Here's another opportunity to express our gratitude for the richness of life itself that Edgar Cayce was wise enough and willing enough to share for our awareness.

CHAPTER 14

Understanding Our Spiritual Nature

Throughout my life, I have had a deep longing to understand the mysteries of the spiritual life, to feel the presence of the Divine. I lost contact with that longing at times, but found that it always returned, and, like the Hound of the Baskervilles, it kept chasing me—seeking me out and demanding answers.

After fifty years of studying and working in the field of medicine, that longing is still there, and it sometimes gives me difficulties, especially when it concerns the healing of the physical body.

Why is it, I questioned my inner self, that we have physical ailments in this dimension when we are really spiritual beings, having eternal life, and the destiny to be one with the Father? Why can't we simply think health, and presto! the body is healed? Our mind is part of our soul body so this should work, right?

We do know that if the therapy offered as treatment for the body is right, healing comes, and often in a matter of hours. I told this story earlier, but it's worth repeating. A child was ill with a high fever, having traveled a long distance that day. It appeared to be a respiratory infection, but we had no medications handy to offer the parents. They did have some Glycothymoline (a common mouthwash which Cayce recommended often to alkalinize the body). Using only six drops in water three times that evening and during the night, the child was perfectly normal the next day, and remained well throughout the week.

This may not have much to do with our spiritual nature, but on the other hand, it could. What if I had a lot of faith in what would happen? And suppose the parents had a similar strong faith? The results may have come through the faith applied, a spiritual quality lodged deep in the soul. We do know that the pH of the body was changed, ever so little, and we know, too, that the immune system functions more normally when the pH is raised just a tiny bit. But is that what Cayce would call a vibratory change? Is that what is needed in healing?

A woman came to the clinic one day with a paralysis of the left side of her face. It was obviously a Bell's Palsy, a neurological condition found frequently when one side of the face has been exposed to the wind, as in driving a car with the window open. She was given one treatment with the acuscope (an electrical transcutaneous therapeutic device) which lasted about thirty minutes, and the paralysis was gone! Normally, through conventional channels, the paralysis may not leave for weeks, and is sometimes permanent.

Could this be the attuning of the atomic structure of the living cellular force to its spiritual heritage as Cayce would say? Does this tell us something about our spiritual nature?

A sixty-eight-year-old woman wrote me about her experience with a condition in both her elbows that has been called "tennis elbow." She went on to create her own "vibratory" kind of treatment program, consisting of "soaking the elbows in a very hot solution of Epsom salts, massaging the painful area with peanut oil, and applying a peanut oil pack and heating pads for a couple of hours. Just two such treatments," she said, "and I regained the full use of my arms in every respect."

We must be vibratory in both our spiritual and physical forms, for each substance found here in this earth environment is composed of atoms, and each atom is vibratory in its nature. This is not limited to electricity and its effects, but is part of each therapy given to an individual, since all medicines, all drugs, all herbs, as well as all mechanical devices, are made of atoms, and are thus vibratory.

Perhaps the vibratory nature of electricity—which Cayce said is not God, but the *manifestation* of God—gives us further bits of understanding about our spiritual nature. We must be in our eternal state (our soul body) a finer vibratory force, for we are indeed like unto God, created in His image. Throughout the Cayce material, God is sometimes called the Creative Forces or Creative Energies. If we are truly fashioned in God's image, then we must also be creative energies or forces.

So can the spiritual "thought"—the prayer that one offers or the faith that one manifests—bring healing? Is that truly a vibration? Evidence concerning this type of event is common in world literature and in the experience of nearly every individual in the earth today. Healing by touch is just about as common.

Two thousand years ago, Jesus touched two blind men's eyes and they could see (Matt. 9:29). A woman touched the hem of His garment (Matt. 9:20-22), and was healed of a chronic uterine hemorrhage. He spoke a word, and the daughter of the ruler of the Synagogue—although she was dead—arose (Mark 5:35-43).

The belief, the faith, the prayer, the word, the touch, the peanut oil, the electric current—all these carry with them healing vibrations, which, if accepted within the consciousness of the body itself, provide for the body a new and better state of health.

Within our soul's memory patterns are instances of this sort of thing coming about in one incarnation or another. It is part of the nature of the soul itself, and we need to recognize it and claim that part of our heritage, given to us in the beginning.

Minor ailments can often give us insights into what causes more significant disabilities. Warts are seldom serious problems to those who find them appearing on some portion of their skin. In several of his readings, Edgar Cayce pursued the problem of warts with a variety of suggestions. His basic premise, however, was that warts came into existence because of a disturbance in the electrical or electromagnetic patterns of the body, most often occurring in childhood. It was almost—as I understand his comments—as if the electric pattern of the body got a bit disrupted, perhaps from a thought form from the unconscious mind, perhaps from an environmental perturbation, or whatever, and the end result was the occurrence of a strange growth, usually toward the end of the extremities, which we call a wart.

Cayce himself, at a conscious level, was often able to get rid of warts for other people simply by touching them with his finger. And he gave some very unusual other suggestions to dissipate these troublesome growths.

An English physician reported many years ago in one of the medical journals how he "bought" warts from his pediatric population at sixpence each. He would hold the coin in the child's hand and say, "Now you know that when you take this money the warts will belong to me?" The children would vigorously nod their heads, take the money, and in three days, as the doctor had earlier instructed them, the warts were gone.

Gordon Sauer, professor of dermatology at the University of Kansas School of Medicine, suggested another method of removal more in line with the Cayce concepts: "Apply a drop or two of castor oil to the wart and cover it with adhesive tape. Tell the patient to leave the tape on for twenty-four hours and to reapply oil and tape daily until the wart is gone . . . Have the patient do this for eight weeks, or until the wart is gone."

The question here, of course, is how does a wart make its appearance? If Cayce is right, it is a disturbance of an electrical nature in the substance of the skin. Well, assuming it is that, and also assuming that suggestion can help the patient rid himself of the wart, then we still must ask how the patient created such a disturbance. The answer is not easy to come by, of course, but something in his electrical/neurological/thought makeup certainly did cause the disturbance. And the finger of the healer sent it off to oblivion. And, most likely, several kinds of treatment might bring about the same results as the castor oil did. We are learning more about the use of electricity in healing the body in these times, but much is still mysterious about how the body can generate or receive these healing impulses.

We still want to know, however, what it is that causes illnesses. Did the child, for instance, create a habit pattern of response from repeated use of an attitude or feeling that brought about a very minimal discord in the electricity and the consciousness of the skin? Somewhere in this incarnation or one in the distant past? Or was it a disturbance brought about while he was still in utero?

One of my patients was complaining that her problem was really her parents. They had mistreated her, emotionally abused her, and she could not help but hate them. Her physical problems were probably to be found in her adrenal glands and the emotions derived from those points in consciousness—the place where her allergies and hypoglycemia had found a home. And she had adopted the familiar stance that "I didn't make myself ill. It's not my fault!"

I reminded her of something I had told her earlier—that Edgar Cayce had said that other people are often like puppets in our lives, like actors on a stage, performing for our benefit. And, in reality, the play is within our own beings, our conscious and unconscious minds, our memories, and in the feelings and thoughts we have created in this and other lifetimes. Repetition of a response or reaction can create strong thought forms in our minds—the puppets Cayce mentioned. And they are all part of our own being and need to be understood, forgiven, and loved.

I reminded her that the other persons whom we criticize or dislike are like mirrors, showing us parts of ourselves, to give us opportunities to understand or to forgive.

She didn't like that idea. But she listened. It is difficult to make a change in attitude as dramatic as this—to see others as playing roles in our theater of life, whether it is as puppets, mirrors, or actors on the stage, as really parts of ourselves, and then to simply understand and love those parts. It always helps, in such an instance, to forgive the other person, while remembering that what we are really forgiving is a part of ourselves that has not measu.~ up to our ideal, as we understand it.

At another time, Cayce put cause and correction into one portion of a reading. He talked about life and its activity in the human body:

> For Life is divine, and each atom in a body that becomes cut off by disease, distrust or an injury, then only needs awakening to its necessity of coordination, cooperation with the other portions that are divine, to FULFILL the purpose for which the body, the soul, came into being. [1173-7]

My patient, who hated her parents at first, realized that she could look at that situation from a different perspective—she could truly forgive her parents—and the healing of her body might follow. For the internal secreting endocrine glands and the body's physiology can start the healing process. Openmindedness is the first step in acquiring not only the understanding needed, but the wisdom that comes through application of that understanding.

Finding the source, then, of a physical difficulty, in an earlier period of her life where relationships were difficult, helped her make a correction, although it did not mandate that this would come about. She realized that the way she had been treated by her parents in this lifetime mirrored the way she had designed her own life to act in relationship to others in prior incarnations.

It's very important to find those basic causes of our troubles, and in doing that search, we will discover that most of these beginnings lie in the realm of fractured relationships. My patient's illnesses and depressions, which she had attributed to her parents, were in reality self-induced, so she could begin to understand that in situations like the ones she experienced with her parents, she needed to learn how to love and bring about harmony, rather than discord. A life lesson, brought about the hard way.

It was more than a quarter of a century ago that I had my first experience with the world of angels, although at the time I didn't see the angelic beings. I was convinced, however, that what was happening had to be something not found within the normal scope of things. I was driving my old Porsche from Monterey Peninsula to Phoenix. It was 1971. There was no real speed limit across the reaches of the California desert, and I was taking advantage of that, for I was in a hurry to complete the 550-mile trip that day. My car had been double-checked before we went to California, but I did not realize that the mechanic had not checked the tires. In those days tires had inner tubes.

The trip across the desert in late July was hot—temperatures ranging from 103 to 115 degrees. Everything seemed uneventful (although very hot) until we reached Wickenburg, just fifty miles from home. Moving along there, inside town, we were traveling at twenty-five to thirty-five miles per hour. We reached the east side of town and suddenly a tire blew out.

I pulled over to the curb and took the wheel off. That was when I believed that there really are angels. The tread on the tire was completely gone—worn out—and in seven different places along the circumference of the tire casing there were holes where I could see the inner tube. The holes were from half an inch in diameter to an inch and a half. I could just imagine seven different angels each holding a hand over one of those holes as our car sped eighty miles an hour over that hot desert highway.

I don't see angels even now. But my friends tell me about their experiences. One of my friends was out in her backyard one day. Her grass had just been cut and she was trying to get a plastic bag filled with grass up and into her trash can. She tried and tried, but it was just too heavy, and she resorted at last to the source she always depended on. She looked up to heaven and cried out with tears in her eyes, "God, I really need help—I really do. Please send someone who can lift this stuff for me!" She no sooner opened her eyes than she heard this voice saying, "Can I help you, ma'am?" She turned around and there was a man standing beside her. She knew her gate to the driveway was locked and no one was in the house—she knew that, but she didn't hesitate. She showed him what she was trying to do. He lifted the bag with ease, and moved the trash can over toward the gate. When my friend turned around to thank the man, there was no one there. She ran into the house, but no one was there either. He was gone. She ran out into the driveway, but not a sight of anyone. My friend was well acquainted with angels, but they most always catch her by surprise. She knew this was another one of those times.

But this is a subject you might better pursue in depth elsewhere. Today there are literally dozens of books, television shows, and magazine articles dealing with one aspect or another of the subject of angels.

The magic in our being doesn't stop, however, with angels. Edgar Cayce talked about Universal Sources of information. He was able to reach outside his own unconscious mind into the source of all information and bring it to our awareness with speech. Consciously he did not remember what he said. And obviously he told about happenings and experiences that he never took part in, either in this life or in past lives. So his outreach was not just into his unconscious mind, the way we have been looking at it.

Someone asked him once what the source of his information was, and he simply said, "Universal Sources." It is important to recognize, however, that the reason he was able to do this kind of work is to be found in his commitment to God, whom he deeply wanted to serve; his past life experiences where he underwent difficulties gave him the strength and the ability to leave his body and enter with a part of his mind into a dimension that is far more expansive than the one we live in. And, while there, he had the ability to gather information.

His ability to do this work also derived from his willingness to submit his body to be used by others so they could be helped. And I think it is fair to say that the ability to give these readings was due also to his obedience to certain Universal Laws—all of which speak of the application of love in its various aspects.

The promise, mostly unrecognized by all of us, of course, is that—given that we become obedient to those same laws and ful-fill the obvious training sessions found in lifetimes of service to God—we, too, might give such readings, if we desire to do so, or reach into the Universal Sources of knowledge and wisdom in some other way. This is not beyond our reach. Of course, we must ask ourselves why we want to do it, and also, is it important that we do it? Too, what will we do with the information when and if we achieve it? Not only did Cayce indicate that this could be done, but Jesus told his disciples essentially the same thing, al-though what he said was more comprehensive and far-reaching than that. He said, "In truth, in very truth, I tell you, he who has faith in me will do what I am doing; and he will do greater things still because I am going to the Father." And then He added a promise, "Indeed, anything you ask in my name I will do . . ." (John 14:12–13).

We could look at these possibilities as if we, in this moment of time, could tap a dimension that is timeless and could experience a bit of the magic that is truly in our own being. Perhaps, for most of us, this moment in time needs to be put into the future, after we have met certain standards. But the promise is there, and we would do well to grasp that promise and let it help us move into the future.

We do know, however, that the ability to delve into these un-known reaches of the mind does not guarantee that we will thus successfully complete our search for healing. That seems to be an-other matter. For illness, we must remember, is not only of the body but of the mind and of the spirit. Despite this complexity, however, the search is worthy of the effort anyone might wish to expend.

CHAPTER 15

Faith and Illness

Karmic influences must ever be met, but He has prepared a way that He takes them upon Himself, and as ye trust in Him, He shows thee the way to meet the hindrances or conditions that would disturb thee in any phase of thine experience. For karmic forces are: What is meted must be met. If they are met in Him that is the Maker, the Creator of all that exists in manifestation, as He has promised, then not in blind faith is it met—but by the deeds and the thoughts and the acts of the body, that through Him the conditions may be met day by day . . .

*No karmic debts from other sojourns or experiences enter in the present that may not be taken away in that, "Lord, have Thy ways with me. Use me as thou seest fit that I may be one with Thee." *442-3

It has been the destiny of the soul that has been separated from the Creator to make contact with Him in efforts to bring about healing of the body. Thus prayer and meditation have been used over the centuries—ever since man took his place on this planet. It is not likely that anyone would pray unless he had faith that there was someone there who was listening. Faith, then, is part of the depths of every individual, for at that level, the soul that has departed from the face of its God knows the nature of the love that awaits him, and he longs to know the richness and the depths of that love. It is the lack of conscious faith and awareness of the God-human relationship that brings on illness. In the same manner, the development of conscious faith—the very nurturing of it—through putting it into action, through prayer and meditation, brings true healing of one's illness.

I received a letter from one of my out-of-town patients who lived through such an experience, and it shows how health might be almost instantaneously restored:

"Please forgive my belated holiday greeting, but two weeks before Christmas I was rushed to the emergency room with a severe asthma attack. It's truly a scary feeling to leave the office early in the day with a minor head cold and wind up calling 911 late that night with some genuine doubts as to whether you're going to be around to see the next sunrise. But that's what happened, and I've been in a state of disbelief ever since.

"There were a lot of folks who cared. Their many and varied kindnesses let me know that I was in their hearts and in their prayers.

"I'm not really sure exactly what prayers are, but I've had a lot of time to think about it. Maybe when you hold a loving and caring thought in your mind about someone, even for just an instant, and recognize that there is a love and a power greater than all of us that truly wants to be called on to help—maybe that's a genuine and valid prayer. I sort of think of us humans as being like electrical transformers where we have the ability (or better yet, the privilege) of receiving God's Love and then directing it where we think it will do the most good.

"Well, however prayer works, the ones that were sent my way were obviously good enough, because I made it and I feel truly blessed."

This man has told me how important faith is in his life, and how he knows those prayers that were sent his way brought about the healing that he experienced.

So how is it that we could best become aware of these abilities within ourselves, and make that relationship with God more real in our lives? There is a quote from the *Library Series Book #23*, p. 308 (A.R.E. Press) that repeats, in a different manner, what has been discussed earlier in this book. But it is so very important that it needs to be emphasized.

This is what Cayce said:

> *As we have given as to how a soul becomes conscious, aware, of its contact with the universal-cosmic-God-Creative Forces in its experience; by feeding upon the food, the fruits, the results of Spirit, of God, of Life, of Reality: love, hope, kindness, gentleness, brotherly love, patience.*
>
> *These make for the awareness in the soul of its relationship to the Creative Force that is manifest in self, in the ego, in the I AM of each soul, and of I AM THAT I AM.*
>
> *So may the entity, the soul of this entity, become aware—through meditating upon those understandings, those truths that are as examples, as witnesses in the earth and its environs—of that which magnifies the Spirit in the earth of the first manifestation of that man calls God and His holy angels . . .* [378-14]

We grow in awareness of the Creative Forces even when we don't quite understand it. If we are gentle, it happens. If we are kind to another person, it happens. If we are patient with the driver of another car trying to get to work, that awareness grows. And it becomes, more and more, a healing force. These qualities are so interlinked with faith and health that it has been difficult for us to believe it. Thus comes the illness, to give us the lesson in faith, in belief, in healing that we need because we did not believe in the first place.

Early in my career in medicine, I avoided taking care of those people who had arthritis, for I knew it would be a long, long time before I could reasonably expect any kind of hopeful results. I was impatient—I wanted results now!

After I began to understand the body differently, I saw the possibilities in helping those with arthritis, for I'd begun to understand that the primary problem is not the swollen and aching joints, but instead a blocking of the channels of elimination.

Arthritis truly is a disease of faulty function in the organs that dispose of body wastes. And in the process of helping those who are involved in this kind of problem, I've also learned a degree of patience. Time and experience has a way of teaching us these important lessons.

Whatever the difficulty, however—whether it be arthritis or the common cold—it always takes time to help the body back to a state of balance, to restore the health that was there before the onset of the disease. Even when a healing of a spiritual nature takes place—and many of these seem to be instantaneous—there is a change that has to happen, and passage of time occurs.

There's a story in *Guideposts* (May 1982, page 342) about a young woman who was severely ill with multiple sclerosis. She was wheelchair-bound, used oxygen continuously, was very weak, and her doctors gave her a very grave prognosis. She loved her church and was deeply disappointed when her illness caused her to give up her work in the church. Then someone suggested that she could really do work at home. She could pray for others who needed help! This excited her, and she followed the suggestion and continued to work this way.

One day, and this was after she had been home-bound for nearly two years, she was visited by two of her girl friends. They were talking when suddenly she heard another voice that said to her "Get up and walk!" She knew it was God talking to her. She called for her mother and father, and then actually stood up and walked. She was totally normal in all regards.

Even this event, given its validity, took time, although the time span must have been simply moments as we count time here. Think of the changes in her physiology and the structure of her body that had to be accomplished! Amazing story, but the changes were even more amazing. Her legs, for example, had been spindly from disuse. All at once, they were well formed, as they had been before the girl became ill. Her mother checked her legs immediately, and the evidence was there in front of her. That night, they went to the church meeting and her minister was shocked and delighted at what had happened to this lovely girl. It leaves most of us in a quandary, for we would be inclined to disbelieve the story. Yet the healing did occur. If the Divine was involved, who can deny what the possibilities are? If there is a God, then we are energy/spiritual/physical bodies and are alive through the grace of God. We have a little sign in our office. It shows a small, rotund man laughing his head off, and above him is the question "God can't do what?" Faith, then, leads us to many wonderful things.

Most people with whom I have talked about sin have resisted the whole idea. Perhaps this is because all people feel that they have only been doing things that have been right, or close to it, and sin carries with it the idea of damnation or exclusion from the grace of God, or something of a similar nature, like, for instance, that we don't know what we are doing.

Scholars who have spent their lives searching the scriptures of the Christian religion see sin as being overcome by the birth of Jesus, who, in the years that followed, lived what has been described as a life of loving without blemish, and became the Christ. Scholars, of course, vary in their opinions. And this is not to take issue with their research or ultimate opinions.

Cayce agrees with the experts, but also takes it a bit deeper. In his readings sin from past lives is dealt with as karma, the law of cause and effect. And to one enquirer, Cayce pointed out that with Jesus being the pattern we need to follow in order to fulfill our life purposes, it becomes important to know that we can overcome any karmic debt by simply loving our fellow man. In essence, Cayce says that all sin can be "taken away" or dispelled, or forgiven, if we let our ways be His ways.

However, the idea of sin must be dealt with in this book, since my purpose is to work with the concepts of illness and healing found in the Cayce readings, and to understand them as they are merged with the practice of medicine—or, for that matter, with any of the healing professions.

Perhaps the quote from the readings that had the greatest effect

on my thinking was Cayce's statement that all illness is sin lying at
our own doorstep. But the readings had much to say to define sin,
and these became helpful in dispelling in my mind the negative
nature of the word that is defined in Webster as "transgression of
the law of God."

For instance, I came to understand better the law of God—that
God is love, and thus, very simply, if we fail in any instance to love
our fellow man, in whom the very spirit of God dwells, we "sin."
In other words, we miss out on the opportunity to follow the pattern. We miss the mark; we fail to hit the bull's-eye of the target;
we fall off the path that we've tried to follow; we move toward the
darkness, turning away from the light.

There are many ways of understanding that we have sinned
without feeling that our destiny to be one with God is lost, since
the very essence of God is love and forgiveness. In the instance of
the woman who had hated her parents because of what they had
done, forgiveness was a key to the healing process. And forgiveness is part of the definition of love. God always forgives us, no
matter how grievously we think we have missed the mark. But I
comfort myself in my acts of not forgiving at times, and try to help
others in the same regard, by realizing that God's power to forgive
is by all means greater than mine. So I accept His forgiveness, and
have found at the same time that it often brings about a change for
the better in the physical body.

Perhaps the most definitive story in the Bible relating forgiveness of sin to healing of the body is found in Luke 5:17–26. "One
day he was teaching, and Pharisees and teachers of the law were
sitting round. People had come from every village of Galilee and
from Judaea and Jerusalem, and the power of the Lord was with
him to heal the sick. Some men appeared carrying a paralyzed
man on a bed. They tried to bring him in and set him down in
front of Jesus, but finding no way to do so because of the crowd,
they went up on to the roof and let him down through the tiling,
bed and all, into the middle of the company in front of Jesus.

When Jesus saw their faith, he said, 'Man, your sins are forgiven you.'

"The lawyers and the Pharisees began saying to themselves, 'Who is this fellow with his blasphemous talk? Who but God alone can forgive sins?' But Jesus knew what they were thinking and answered them: 'Why do you harbor thoughts like these? Is it easier to say, "Your sins are forgiven you," or to say, "Stand up and walk"? But to convince you that the Son of Man has the right on earth to forgive sins'—he turned to the paralyzed man—'I say to you, stand up, take your bed, and go home.' And at once he rose to his feet before their eyes, took up the bed he had been lying on, and went home praising God. They were all lost in amazement and praised God; filled with awe, they said, 'You would never believe the things we have seen today.'"

So, what *is* the difference—if we were to know that our faith in the loving care of a bountiful God were to heal our bodies or were to forgive our sins? Would it not be that we had turned from darkness to light either way? Or returned from picking daisies to take our place once again on the path toward our goal—a closer oneness with God? We need a deeper study of the situation.

For instance if one had developed unforgiving anger and judgment of those who disagreed with him by repeatedly, in past lives, imprisoning and perhaps even torturing them, it would be residing in his unconscious mind in the present time as a habitual response. He would likely be very judgmental in his relationships this time around. This would be "sin" in Cayce's way of looking at it, since one was not practicing forgiveness.

A healing of this thought form, no matter how it might come about, would very likely be a turning point in the progression of a severe hypertension in an individual who experienced the relief of such a pattern in the inner depths of his unconscious mind. And we could say, "Your sins have been forgiven you—even though it's been done through your acceptance of this concept—

and your high blood pressure is gone. You've been healed physically."

Cayce said to one man that he should remember that it is only self he was meeting that causes anxieties or any character of trouble. And the man was told that the part of himself that he was meeting was the part that failed to follow the whole law that "Thou shalt love the Lord thy God with all thy mind, thy body, thy soul, and thy neighbor—thy brother, thy friend, thy foe—as thyself" (4047-2). But then, he was told that his appearances in the earth were all to give him the opportunity of meeting himself, "For the purpose is that each soul should be a co-creator with God."

Cayce seems to be saying that when an individual is at variance with Divine law, sin enters, and the discord in the body creates dis-ease or disease sooner or later. Fighting does this. Rebellion does this. But we all can change, although we have to know how to go about changing.

In giving readings pertaining to the Search for God study groups—when these were being developed in the early thirties—Cayce told participants that suffering, such as they might experience in an illness, was mercy, a kind of justice for the soul! *"For those things that are cares of the flesh and of the earth cannot inherit eternal life. Hence life alters, life changes in the experiences of individuals through their sojourns in the earth, and thus ye learn thy lessons."* And correction, it seems, is learning *"that God is merciful, is love, is justice, is patience, is long-suffering, is brotherly love; for these are the law, not of the law but the law. And the law is love and the law is God"* (262-100).

Healing of the human body implies that one knows the cause of the illnesses which afflict the body and from which the body needs to be healed. Cayce's insights into the nature of the body bring into focus an etiology that is consistent (as we have already seen) with that identified in the Bible. Both in the readings and in the Old and New Testaments, sickness is really a sickness of the soul and is caused by what has been termed sin. As in this reading, Cayce often gives cause and correction in just a few words:

> For the only sin of man is SELFISHNESS!
>
> Q-8. How may it be overcome?
>
> A-8. Just as has been given; showing mercy, showing grace, showing peace, long-suffering, brotherly love, kindness—even under the most TRYING circumstances.
>
> For what is the gain if ye love those ONLY that love thee? But to bring hope, to bring cheer, to bring joy, to bring a smile again to those whose face and heart are bathed in tears and in woe, is but making that divine love SHINE—SHINE—in thy own soul! 987-4

Still another comment from the readings pointed out that

> the life of a soul must be in the manifesting of the glory of the Father, through the Son, in this material plane. For, other than that makes for selfishness, that is the basis of all sin in the earth. 518-1

In the A.R.E. Clinic, and I'm sure in the offices of doctors throughout the world, a sincere effort is constantly being made to help patients by applying those fruits of the spirit in a healing environment. If selfishness is the only sin, and if sin causes illness, then in the long run, the illness in the souls of those who are aspiring to health cannot be adequately corrected without the giving of a smile from the heart, the kindnesses, the absence of judgment and criticism, the hope that may be generated in the patient's body as mercy, peace, brotherly love, and long-suffering are applied. These are the true elements of healing, and they may be applied by anyone. If these are absent in the office of a doctor or therapist, the best cannot come about. And, by the same token, if the patient refuses to accept them or refuses to manifest these fruits of the Spirit, time often passes without the healing of the body.

So we must ask, Is there a direct relationship between sin and sickness? Jesus knew there was, that essentially sin and sickness

were the same thing. Thus to heal or to forgive sins was to perform the same act. In the Divine picture, we sin when we find ourselves not listening well enough to God's Law. God created us in
His image and wants us to be co-creators with Him, to be one with
Him. So he has a backup kind of a plan, we might say, although
that is putting an earthly term to a Divine thought. Yet, His desire
is to have everyone on the planet finding his way back home, back
to a oneness with Him.

The backup plan is called karma, but how does it fit into the
picture of healing? The power of the unconscious mind and the
emotional centers and the manner in which memory is stored
there and in the very tissues of the body make for an interesting
situation. The relationships of past lives remain with us until we
replace the habits which have caused the turmoil in our present
life with new habit patterns. And we need to remember that repetition of action is what creates habits. So the action has to be repeated over and over again until, as in learning how to type on a
typewriter or a computer, the body and the body's consciousness
have learned the lesson.

When we meet conditions in the physical world, we are simply
experiencing what we have already created. I had a patient with
an acute sore throat who had driven halfway across the United
States without sleep. He was worried about a sister, ate poorly
while traveling, and he developed an inflamed pharynx, undoubtedly as a result of these influences that are always a detri-
ment to the body. He was worn out, obviously, and his immune
system was suffering. He was meeting in the earth what he had
created. He ignored the rules of health required of the human
body, so he became ill. He learned something about the laws of
the body through that experience. Maybe not much, but *something*.

Karma is a bit different. It deals for the most part with eternal,
spiritual laws, not necessarily those of the earth. We meet ourselves sometimes in a physical illness because we failed in the past

to live the laws of the spirit which we had already come in contact with and accepted. Cayce said,

> *Karma is, then, that that has been in the past builded as INDIFFERENCE to that KNOWN to be right! Taking chances, as it were—"will do better tomorrow—this suits my purpose today—I'll do better tomorrow." Karma is that; making that correction.* [257-78]

But bad karma can be avoided by opening oneself to learning the lesson that was disregarded before. For karma is only another way of learning. By being patient, by being still, by listening, one can find that path toward the light which some call grace.

The idea of the wheel of karma comes from Eastern religions, where it is generally thought that meeting oneself in the law of cause and effect is like a wheel that keeps on going round and round. And we do, of course, keep on meeting ourselves in everything that seems like a difficulty. I don't think we really have fun in living out a karmic situation, but why would we have created this circumstance in the first place if we hadn't felt it was necessary? Maybe we did, indeed, have fun creating that pattern within the depths of our own mind. We are amazing creatures and must admit that we might have really created something that in present time doesn't seem to be reasonable.

Given, however, that there are karmic diseases, can we reverse them? Is this a possibility? My research of the Cayce readings has led me to the conclusion that most serious, long-term, degenerative diseases—like Parkinson's disease, rheumatoid arthritis, amyotrophic lateral sclerosis, and muscular dystrophy—are karmic in nature. Seemingly conflicting viewpoints about the reversibility potential of these diseases can be found in medicine, in world literature, in the Bible, and in the readings.

For the physician, it is important that a conclusion be reached, for this question has a strong bearing on how a patient with such a disease will be treated. For instance, if one carries to a logical conclusion the biblical statement that "He who killeth with the sword must be killed with the sword" (Rev. 13:10), then any karma that afflicts the body must fulfill its course. There are many instances that would lead one naturally to assume that in a real karmic condition it would be fruitless to try to achieve a full return to normal.

However, there is always a point where karma ceases. Since it is really a debt, it can be paid off like any other debt, by higher forces that can bring healing. However, the disease process ends with death of the physical body, so there is a point where karma ends—a place of spiritual understanding where the lessons are well taught and well learned. We might call this point "where karma ends and grace begins." Grace seems to be a point of forgiveness, accepted by the person experiencing the karma. The forgiveness may have been offered for a long time, but acceptance of it may have been delayed. Perhaps this is because of choice on the part of the one who might have accepted the healing. The Cayce material appears to lend credence to the concept that rejection is rebellion and rebellion is sin—as is the disease, expressed as sin lying at your own doorstep.

Acceptance, then, must be—in this way of thinking—a portion of the healing process, and must be a part of the spiritual learning that an entity undergoes during the time he spends on the earth.

In the case of a person with Parkinson's disease who had asked about building immunity, Cayce suggested electrical therapy to enhance the immune system, but added that

Even karmic forces will be met in definite spiritual purposes. 3011-2

Under those circumstances, one who is afflicted with an "incurable disease" is challenged to recognize that, at any moment, he may have learned the lesson inherent in the experience, and he may at that point be healed. For the debt may have been excused—for, after all, the whole karmic experience is a backup plan to make sure that the spiritual lesson is not only accepted, but also learned. The forgiving of the debt is grace entering into that person's life, and a part of his adventure in consciousness.

But, most often, of course, we don't remember past life situations and don't even recognize a disease as being karmic in origin. Still and all, where there has been misuse of our opportunities simply to love our fellow man, we have made a deposit in our unconscious mind that must be paid back or played back—like an audiotape—at a later time. And this is a Universal Law. We can certainly feel empathy toward another who is experiencing his karma, but we cannot remove it for him. He has to meet it himself. Cayce, however, stated over and over again that anyone can meet that situation with the Christ as a companion, and then it simply doesn't hurt as much. It's met in a different way, which is most easily understood as grace, or forgiveness.

We have built habit patterns in the past that were not recognized as being disturbing or destructive, but were only the manifestations of an individual soul that was not yet perfected, that still had quite a ways to go. But we built these patterns with the mind using the power of choice to direct our actions. Keeping in mind the idea that we are body, mind, and spirit (or soul) here in the earth, then we remember that the mind is the builder.

The mind is indeed a powerful tool for creating, constructing, and forming not only habits in the unconscious mind, but "real" things in this material world. We are constantly creating new habits, or else making more solid and permanent the old ones. If they are helpful in our lives and in the lives of other people, then they are of the spirit. If not, they partake of the flesh and are not in the nature of what we call God, for they are destructive. God is loving, constructive, helpful, and through those activities that we call "good," builds in our lives and in our bodies healthy relationships and health of the physical body.

We become channels for one or the other, as we react to people and situations in life, and thus build either a God-likeness in our being, or else a condition that is destructive in our functioning bodies, as well as relationships in our daily lives that bring turmoil and warring. In the world as a whole we see these kinds of emotions and attitudes manifesting as either peace or warfare. If all of us in the planet earth were to act out our destiny that Jesus suggested when he said "Ye are gods" (John 10:34) we would all be bringing light and peace to the world.

So what do we individually do about it? Perhaps the direct answer is to choose according to our ideal which way we want to go and then check with our higher source, the Christ within. Because often our ideal is not the one that the Creative Forces have in mind for us.

Seek in the mental mind the answer to all questions that may be presented in the things that may be thy experiences day by day, and have the answer within self as thou prayest. Then lay this answer before the Throne of grace, or mercy itself, as thou would meditate within the chambers of thine own heart, and the answer will be within self as to the necessary step, the necessary things to perform to be rid of the warring of the flesh with the spirit. While each body, each soul in the flesh is subject to the flesh, yet—as has been given of Him, "Though ye may be in the world, ye may not be of this world, if ye will put your whole trust, your whole love, your whole life, in His keeping." He will not lead thee astray. He will guide, guard and direct thee, even as has been given, "He loveth every one and giveth his own life for those that will come to Him."

In the preparations, then, for these warrings within, as has been given, meet them step by step. That that is given thee put to use, for only in the use of that which is thine own may this grow, even as patience and mercy and love and endurance and tolerance. Putting them to use they become those bulwarks that prevent an interception from carnal forces or the spirits of an evil influence. For, these are helpless in HIS sight; for He is made Lord of all. 442-3

We must learn how to love, in order that we might meet ourselves within that law of karma in a different way. Then we realize we have been shown some Divine kindness and have learned the lesson. And I've often felt that it is more meaningful to us if we acknowledge, when we are facing something we do not like, that it is the result of what we have sown in the past. At that point, we are called upon to face ourselves in a forgiving attitude and even find the joy in recognizing that we are learning yet another portion of the Divine Law.

So, back to some questions: Did our parents, for instance, "give" us this illness that is currently taking its toll in our body? No, not really. Don't forget that we all chose our parents this incarnation, before we were born. And we are probably reaping some of what we have sown somewhere in the past.

And are we "supposed" to get sick? Is there a purpose to it? Yes, there is a purpose to it. All this information seems to be saying that illness is part of the plan of making us more one with the Creative Forces of the Universe, an opportunity to learn how to treat our fellow man. There is a treasure to be discovered, beyond the obvious, in meeting ourselves in our search. The kind of thing that has been called "diamonds in our own backyard."

And, too, I should ask, What part did I play in this illness of my physical body? Didn't someone else at least help to cause it? Can't I blame someone? My parents, my boss, maybe even God, who created me in the first place? Well, no, we cannot blame someone else, if we are going to follow these suggestions about what illness really means in our search for healing here in the earth. We become healthier if we take responsibility for our own being, seeing that we have infinite potential, given us from our very creation, and, as Cayce reminds us again and again, there are no conditions of illness that cannot be brought back to normal. And normal means a state of health.

However, it is wise to recall to our minds that even though we cannot blame someone else for the illness we are experiencing, we should not blame ourselves, either, for blame does nothing of value. Instead, we can recognize that the pain we are feeling or the discomfort is only a call to action in learning another lesson on the way to our destiny.

CHAPTER 16

Tapping into Our Spiritual Energy

If each of us lives in a sort of universe of his own, as Cayce seems to point out—for we are born by ourselves and we die by ourselves—then we need to pull together the various aspects of what influences us to bring us to the point where we are sick. And we have been finding bits and pieces of the solution here in this book as we make our way along.

Many factors have had a part to play in this picture of illness, but there are also capabilities within us that can play a major role in bringing about a healing, and even a level of health that spells regeneration, rejuvenation, and longevity. All of these factors are probably active within each of us at the present time, but in varying degrees of strength or excellence.

In earlier chapters, I've discussed our origin and nature as souls spending time in the earth plane, reincarnating over and over again from the spiritual dimension. Also the power of choice has been touched on. The manner in which the autonomic nervous system plays its part in the coordination of functions in the body has been dealt with to an extent; and the method that has been created (as the sensory nervous system) to allow the body to be aware of itself in the material plane; as well as the way the cerebrospinal nervous system allows us to become active in doing things—all of these have been touched on.

We have also worked with the relationship between the conscious and unconscious minds, and the manner in which habits or thought forms or automatic responses are brought into being. But we haven't yet put it all together in answering adequately the question Why am I sick—what happened?

If you review again the chart of symbolic meanings associated with the seven spiritual/glandular centers that have been recorded over the centuries (Table 1), you can understand better that these seven points of awareness must always be dealt with in searching for healing—especially when we see the hormones involved and the emotional patterns that might play a part in the illness.

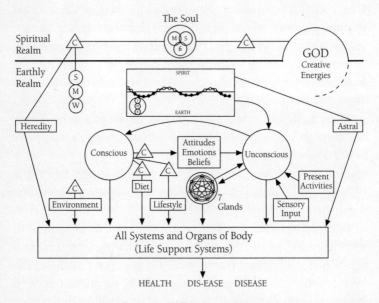

DIAGRAM 7. THE BIG PICTURE.

I've put together in Diagram 7 much of the information that has already been used as diagrams. But I've also added other concepts, and I've tried to show how choices that we make daily play a major role in health and disease.

The symbology of the seven circles within the larger circle shows how these seven endocrine centers relate to one another and take a place in the scheme of things relating to both aspects of the mind—the conscious and unconscious—and to the physical functioning body.

One of the obvious facts is that each human being is fashioning today what his future will probably be. In the same manner he fashioned things in all those past lives. We come to earth every time with the same basic tools, the same soul body and the same ability to choose. The choice, of course, makes the difference. For always there is the choice between what Cayce calls self-aggrandizement, and its opposite, the desire to serve our fellow man. One direction looks at self, the other at the God-part in the other fellow.

In every incarnation, the transition is made from the spiritual realm to the physical or earth plane, and as the child grows, he learns that he can make decisions, or choose certain things. The capacity is allowed to blossom as the individual goes through the early years, the interim period between childhood and adulthood, and from that point on the choice is his in every instance in fashioning his life.

He may not recognize that fact throughout his lifetime, but it remains a fact, and needs to be understood—it is God's most precious gift to him, and he cannot find his way back home without exercising it over and over again. Moses told the Children of Israel that it was up to them to make choices. He said, "For this commandment which I command thee this day, it is not hidden from thee, neither is it far off. It is not in heaven, that thou shouldest say, 'Who shall go up for us to heaven, and bring it unto us, that we may hear it, and do it?'

"Neither is it beyond the sea, that thou shouldest say, 'Who shall go over the sea for us, and bring it unto us, that we may hear it, and do it?' But the word is very nigh unto thee, in thy mouth, and in thy heart, that thou mayest do it.

"See, I have set before thee this day life and good, and death and evil; in that I command thee this day to love the Lord thy God, to walk in his ways, and to keep his commandments and his statutes and his judgments, that thou mayest live and multiply: and the Lord thy God shall bless thee in the land whither thou goest to possess it" (Deuteronomy 30:11–16).

Later on in this thirtieth chapter of Deuteronomy, Moses said the same thing in a different way. "I call heaven and earth to record this day against you, that I have set before you life and death, blessing and cursing; therefore choose life, that both thou and thy seed may live; that thou mayest love the Lord thy God, and that thou mayest obey his voice, and that thou mayest cleave unto him: for he is thy life and the length of thy days" (Deuteronomy 30:19, 20).

It is in the conscious state that the will is exercised, that choices are made, so it is up to us to use that left brain of ours and make choices, so the way might be made as clear ahead of us as we can understand it to be. Then we can claim one of the promises from the Cayce readings, that the attempt to do good is held by God to be righteousness. And we are then on the path, despite the stumbling that may slow down our progress.

In Diagram 7, the conscious mind is unable to control the sensory input from day to day—we are in a material world. But we must remember that we chose where we are going to be, no matter how we might have allowed others to influence our choices. By allowing others to move us, we allow that sensory input to happen. We cannot often control the events that happen around us and impact our sight and hearing—but we do have control over how we respond inside and outside to those events.

What we do in our life situations generally is probably in the same category. We do what we choose to do. When the boss tells us to do something, we usually do it. But we chose to take that job in the first place, and the boss goes with it. If we don't want to follow the boss's orders, we don't need to. We can quit and find another job. All of this, of course, depends on our choices.

And we need to remind ourselves over and over again that we did this same thing with our ability to choose in all those past lives. Those choices took us places that today we would not go. But then, we were in a different environment and had to function in that place and time.

In Diagram 7, we chose to enter the earth, and our conscious mind chooses what kinds of emotions we exercise into habits. We keep seeing those people—those mirrors—that I mentioned earlier, and they give us opportunities to devise different kinds of emotional patterns if we choose to do so.

The unconscious mind reacts; it does not make choices. Neither do the emotions, locked up in those seven centers of hormonal activity. They follow orders, too, until the order to change is given repeatedly, and the kind of change is indicated. Then it can happen, and it does happen.

As I have mentioned earlier, there always seems to be a battle going on inside the human body. If there truly is peace, associated with love, in its full aspect, then the battles are all history, and the olive branch has been accepted by both sides. But, we ask, what are the two sides that are most often in conflict with each other? Where do they reside, and what is the nature of the warfare? There are probably several ways of looking at this very important question.

First of all, we need to consider that we are all spiritual beings—souls—making a journey through the earth. So the conflict, the war, would naturally be the spiritual nature against the material, or earth, nature. We are urged to overcome the earth, but we find it difficult. Sooner or later there comes the disturbance, when one of us desires deeply to take the high road, the Path of Light, and move toward oneness with God. And all this at a conscious, seeking level. Then the patterns and desires and wants of the world we know so well rise up and try to destroy that which is of light and hope and love. We attempt to tap into our spiritual energy and the war begins.

It could be much as Paul once said of himself: "For the good that I would [do] I do not: but the evil which I would not, that I do. Now if I do that I would not, it is no more I that do it, but sin that dwelleth in me. I find then a law, that, when I would do good, evil is present with me. For I delight in the law of God after the inward man. But I see another law in my members, warring against the law of my mind, and bringing me into captivity to the law of sin which is in my members" (Romans 7:19–24).

Later on, Paul had this to say:

"Those who live on the level of our lower nature have their outlook formed by it, and that spells death; but those who live on the level of the spirit have the spiritual outlook, and that is life and peace" (Romans: 8:5–6).

From my studies of Paul's writings as presented in the New Testament, and the suggestions about healing from Edgar Cayce's psychic readings, I have found that the two individuals are very closely aligned as to what sin might be—missing the mark as we do things in this world, or following our own wants and desires as we relate to our fellow human beings. In a sense, failing to live up to the Law of Light and Love, and doing our own thing instead.

Prior to that kind of awakening, however, and if the search has not yet started, life goes on in the same old way. And the wars we fight in our bodies are not major world conflicts. They can be treated and stopped with an aspirin tablet, a massage or manipulation, or even a stronger medication of one sort or another. Or, perhaps, just a kind word. But the urge to move upward has not died. It is just in hibernation, and will arise sooner or later.

Then, when the urge to really live is rekindled, how do we localize where the line of battle exists in mankind? If we choose to look at the figure of a man standing, facing us, we can say that the line of battle is to be found at the level of the top of the shoulders. The three glands above this line—the thyroid, the pineal, and the pituitary—are called the higher centers. Below this line are the four lower centers. And these two groups are always in conflict until the beasts that symbolize the four can show their love and obedience to the Creator, as described in the fourth chapter of the Revelation. The four are described as like a lion, a calf, a beast with a face as a man, and a flying eagle.

"And when these beasts give glory and honor and thanks to him that sat on the throne, who liveth for ever and ever, the four and twenty elders fall down before him that sat on the throne, and worship him that liveth for ever and ever, and cast their crowns before the throne, saying 'Thou art worthy, O Lord, to receive glory and honor and power: for thou hast created all things; and for thy pleasure they are and were created' " (Rev. 4:9–11).

In this scene, there was also a sea of glass, representing stilled emotions, the seven lamps of fire burning before the throne, and, of course, the One who sat on the throne. The beasts are the four lower centers, and the twenty-four elders are the double set of twelve cranial nerves where the senses of the body are located. So it is that not only have the emotions, symbolized by the sea of glass, been stilled, but the seven lamps of fire representing the seven spiritual/endocrine centers are alive and well as the Spirits of the Divine. And the four beasts are celebrating.

When the desires and wants of the lower centers have been let go of, then the senses show their obedience to the One on the throne by giving up their crowns; the emotions have been stilled and the seven centers have come into an attunement with the Divine. In other words, no longer is there a war between the forces on either side of the line of battle. There is peace.

This is part of the great conflict that is happening inside our bodies most all the time, probably more so now than it has for thousands or even millions of years. For a time of reckoning has been seen by many to be coming about within the lifetime of most of us who read this book. Modern-day psychics have predicted it, and it has been documented from a variety of religious sources by those who know and read symbology.

In our Temple Beautiful program, we help people track down

the elements of this battle that shows itself seemingly at odd times. For it has had its beginning somewhere in time past. Cayce said the past is ever there, but set it behind thee! This means, of course, that we need to release it in some manner. But we need to identify what it is that we are going to release, because the emotion is too often hidden from our efforts to seek out and deal with it adequately.

One of the keys to soul growth (toward our oneness with God) is recognizing when another person is acting as a mirror or as a puppet for others in a given situation. This can be for an individual or for several people in a group. In a group situation, some may come to understand what really happened many years ago or even in a past life that brought about the emotional turmoil which in turn gave birth to the bodily changes which in turn grew to become the illness or illnesses that they are now experiencing. In using Diagram 7, it is as though one is playing detective, placing the disease or illness at the bottom, and then working up through the physiological changes to the unconscious mind. For it is there that the cause resides: those patterns, the habits of response from repeated interpersonal relationships that were met in anger or frustration rather than in love. These responses, built into patterns, then brought about the turmoil in the physiology, with the latter ultimately bringing about the disease. Knowledge of the real cause of this difficulty—and acceptance of it—brings a relief and can then be a turning point toward healing of the spirit.

Sometimes we call these interpersonal difficulties stresses. They occur in the home, in the marketplace, in schools, in hospitals, and in the streets. But they *do* occur. And we must remember that they are only—and always—reactions from the depths of our own being to what we see in the world outside. And the world outside is saying to us, "This is you, my friend, a part of your consciousness that you just have not understood previously, that is found within your own body and mind." So the world becomes a teacher and a mirror. Our adversary is a puppet, playing its part in our lives to remind us that what we are fighting is really us, and we have not yet arrived at the state that is called oneness with the Creative Forces of the Universe. The Cayce legacy tells us we would best find the joy in each of these occasions, for they are there for us, and for our learning, and we can do it with celebration and happiness if we choose.

Often the discovery of an emotional or attitudinal block gives us a wider view of ourselves and, when the discord is set at rest—with love—not only leads to a greater insight into what we really are, but becomes a stepping-stone to healing our physical body.

Our heredity and environment also contribute to our quest for spirituality. Our parents, for example, not only guide us in our formative years to the best of their ability, but also grant to us certain positive traits, physical characteristics, and a host of tendencies, both mental and physical. Too, we are often given weaknesses that can progress to illness over a period of time, for there are a variety of diseases that can be passed on genetically.

We did choose our parents, though, didn't we? And, if our mystical-religion heritage has any reality, we knew before we committed ourselves to these two people that we would have an inheritance that would help to shape our life. We were undoubtedly assisted in choosing the time to come into this life, so the astrological signs would be correct for what we wanted to accomplish.

Once we made the commitment, then, we grew into the kind of infant that had the facial characteristics that were granted to us, the size and shape of our body as a whole, and the kind of internal organs and systems that would suit our purpose. Some have small adrenal glands; others have very large centers of adrenal activity. This is according not only to the parents that we choose, but also to the kind of development that we experienced in those particular adrenal glandular emotions in past lives. What kind of activities did we take part in? Were we warriors and fighters, or were we college professors or accountants? It would not do well for a musician to go out on the football field with three-hundred-pound giants. So we have parents who have prepared themselves to have children who will be able to meet this lifetime in a way that offers them the choices they need. We may fit into the family or not well at all, and this may be one of our life challenges—how we get along with other family members.

It is not reasonable to try and analyze completely why we may have entered into a particular family. But we can do some creative thinking and use our powers of imagination, and see the sense in being where we are. It helps to look again every now and then at Diagram 7. For there we can see how various lifetimes may have shaped our future, and brought into our unconscious minds very strong desires and goals—goals that require specific physical characteristics, which may have drawn us together with our newly chosen parents and made for a most helpful set of experiences.

We might then look at our heredity as part of what we have taken on based on patterns we created in the past, and the source of guideposts and tools for this incarnation.

While our parents and our heredity are chosen from the spiritual side of our existence, the environment we find ourselves in is a combination of the spiritual choices made before birth and those generated by the activity of the conscious mind once in physical reality. Certainly our goals chosen before birth have to be part of where we locate and what kind of a home we finally create. But most of these are the product of conscious choosing. We might say, "Well, that was really what my spouse wanted, and I didn't particularly want to be there." That is OK, but on the other hand, who chose the spouse? Interesting, isn't it, how we come to design, though the operation of God's greatest gift, our environment, good or bad, in the valley or the mountain, in a polluted atmosphere or in the clarity of the open desert? Or our environment might be as a journalist in one of the wars that constantly seem to be our heritage. One might, for a variety of reasons, choose to be one who gets involved in the wars directly by being born in the right country or circumstance. This might be a very difficult life.

And these choices of heredity and environment help to create the kind of a stage on which we play our part in the drama of life. There are benefits and the hardships coming from both of these choices. We always choose the situations that will allow us opportunities for soul growth, and until we become fully aware of what these mean in our lives, we find them to be joining with our unconscious needs to meet ourselves in predetermined karmic situations, and formulating the kinds of illnesses we fall heir to.

If a Beethoven or a Mozart had been born into a family dealing with finance or politics as a major family direction, instead of music, we probably would not have had the masterpieces of classical music that they left us as their legacy. At the same time, each of these two geniuses had to face some very specific problems with his health, which made for him much in the way of suffering.

Life is not just choosing what we do and picking parents we would like to have for this particular incarnation, but that choice does have a very significant effect on what our lives are going to be and, too, what sort of illnesses might come our way.

In answering the question about what brings illness to our bodies, we tend to disregard the most obvious factors. This is probably due to our human nature, so-called, which often moves us to doing what we want to do, rather than what we would best do in order to build health in our body. We find examples everywhere in our daily walks through life. For example, we may need to lose weight. There may be thirty or thirty-five extra pounds we are carrying along as unwanted baggage. But we *like* to eat, and we like to eat those things that are fattening! This may be a pattern. We cannot blame our parents, for instance. We cannot blame our spouses, who may be cooking what they think is best. We really should not even blame ourselves, for blame brings about judgment and we understand the biblical warning "Judge not, that ye be not judged" (Matt. 7:1).

One patient who had a weight problem came to me for help. He was aware of diet and fasting and wanted to go on a juice fast. One suggestion in the Cayce readings was to dilute Welch's grape juice half and half with water and drink that at mealtimes and between meals, if desired. Apparently, there is food sufficient for the human body in grape juice over a long period of time. This man weighed nearly three hundred pounds. He followed the diet over a three-month period and lost about ninety pounds. He remained healthy and working the entire time and maintained his weight at the new level without difficulty. His laboratory findings remained normal throughout. After his weight loss goal was achieved, he followed a diet heavy in vegetables, both fresh and lightly steamed, fruit, and, two or three times a week, fish or fowl. He was easy on the starches and avoided the sweets as much as possible.

While the problem was met and made into a positive part of life for this man, it still becomes a problem often for our bodies to handle, carrying around that much more weight than would keep us in good shape. At the same time we often resist exercising, because we don't have time, or it is raining outside, or it is too cold to exercise, or we just don't feel like it. We have many excuses, but the bottom line is that we often start an exercise program and then give it up when we are challenged to be persistent and consistent and patient.

We frequently stay up too late at night, watching television or going to a show—any one of a hundred things that might be fun to do. It is excellent, of course, to have fun, to laugh and enjoy life. No problem about that. However, when we fail to give ourselves enough sleep time, the body suffers, and inroads are made against one's health. Then we wonder why we develop that cold, or find our bodies aching. Symptoms develop in our lives and we wonder what kind of an illness we are "getting"—when it is only a matter of our abusing those life-support systems within by the manner in which we live our lives.

In Diagram 7, our lifestyle is shown as having an effect on those internal functioning parts of our bodies, but it is also noted that the lifestyle is a product of our choices at a conscious level. We are constantly being bombarded by bits of information from our unconscious minds that might be playing old tapes, old memory patterns, that take precedence over our conscious choices. We allow that to happen, but we usually have an excuse which allows us to keep on going and not think too much about what we are doing to ourselves.

Edgar Cayce spoke about lifestyle before the word came into its present-day usage as far as health is concerned. He made specific suggestions about diet, smoking, drinking, exercise, and balance between work, rest, and recreation. All of these currently are seen as lifestyle choices that have a beneficial or detrimental effect on our state of health.

The Cayce approach is one of balance and moderation, not rigidity or a totally listless approach to life. We know, of course, that a health-producing approach to life often is deserted when one feels sick. This is not surprising, but choice can bring about a turnaround in how one "feels" about things and this in turn often helps in the recovery of health.

When we are dealing with moving the structural body with treatment methods like exercise or massage, manipulation or adjustments, we can understand that one purpose of doing this is simply to keep the spine flexible so that nerve energies, which are really bits of information, might pass through the openings in the spinal vertebrae without being hampered. Since nerve impulses are simply a means of communication, it becomes important that the messages being thus transmitted are clear.

All of these methods of moving the joints, muscles, tendons, and ligaments become part of one's lifestyle, as does the choice of whether one smokes or not, whether alcohol is part of one's life in a casual way or as a way of life itself, and whether one balances sleep, rest, fun, reading, and so on. We truly produce a symphony of activities that all play their part in telling us that we feel "Great!" or more like "Hey, why in the world do I feel so badly? What's going on inside my body?"

It is difficult to follow through on our conscious choices and deny those unconscious blips that sneak up on us when we are not looking. But that is the challenge we face in today's world, and we had better recognize that we can make changes if we really want to. Or we can simply keep on with the kinds of choices that we have made into habits in our deeper mind, and let that part of ourselves go ahead and give us difficulties.

In putting our history into perspective, we need to consider the effects brought to our bodies by what we might call astral influences. We may know more today about what happens on the side of life that we call the spiritual dimension, but the knowledge is still quite limited and often fragmented. Sometimes it is nonexistent—we lack knowledge that we can pin down, as we can strep infection being present in the throat. The streptococcus bacteria, for example, is a part of this earth environment, but when we investigate the spirit domain much of what exists there escapes our scrutiny.

Some who have retained memories of the spiritual dimension say we may go to universities on the other side. Some believe that they will go to hell when they die, but if they have had a near death experience, they have a permanent change of mind, and know that they can look forward to that death/birth with gladness, for the experience has given them a wonderful promise.

There are relationships that occur between incarnations, according to those who have reason to know. But it seems that there is almost always some learning that will be helpful for the entity when he is aided again across the border to be born into the earth plane. The influences, however, will be of assistance in helping the individual find his purpose in the upcoming life in the earth, and meet the physical challenges in the most successful manner.

Cayce often indicated that we come into this life from one of the other planets in this solar system, or from the environment of the sun or the moon, bringing with us the influences that are found to be consistent with that planet in the language of astrology.

It seems that the influences from that area of life appear more as urges, feelings within one, and seem to move one in a direction without understanding why. Cayce had the following to say about these urges and how they become part of us:

In analyzing the records here of this entity, there are many urges latent and manifested in the experience. The entity oft finds itself efficient, but somewhat officious unto those that are in the environ of the entity . . .

Astrologically we find urges, not according to astrological terminology; but as ye are in this solar system ye are subject to the laws thereof. And the planets, the constellations, the sun and the moon each have their environs or their influences, dependent upon the manner of the entity's manifestation in same. Just as the environ of any section of the country carries with it the soliloquies of that particular portion of the country, so does the environ or consciousness of the entity as a whole carry with it the influence from its sojourn in that consciousness represented by the sun and moon, Mars and Jupiter, Venus and Neptune; according to the use which the entity has made of its experiences . . . [3299-1]

When we have had many incarnations in the earth, we have become even more complex as individuals. Not only have we accumulated more habit patterns of attitudes which become part of how we relate with others, but the urges that we take on through our association with planets of this solar system give us nuances of character and personality which help to make us totally different from all other beings on the planet. But the differences make for a more interesting set of experiences for all of us as we travel that path we have chosen toward our destiny. We each have a particular set of challenges which give us the opportunity to love one another or to move in the opposite direction. Here's an example of how one of our Temple Beautiful patients tapped into her spiritual energy to forgive herself.

Jean mentioned that in waking life she had always loved clean new notebooks, and when they got marked up a bit, she would discard them. Then she had this dream in which she was standing in an outdoor setting, and in front of her stood Jesus. He looked different from what she had thought He would look like, but she had never dreamed of him before. Both Jean and Jesus were surrounded and enveloped in a glorious white light in the dream.

Jesus had a tattered, beat-up old notebook in his hand which she thought was really terrible looking. He set it aside for a moment and reached down to the ground and picked up a large boulder, which left a hole in the earth. Bright light streamed from the hole. Jesus placed the old notebook in the streaming light for a moment, then picked it up and gave it to her. It was totally new, bright and beautiful. End of the dream.

You can gain some clues about the meaning of the dream by researching a bit in the book of John (1:4–9) and Revelation (10:7–11). Light, you know, is the Christ and is cleansing. The book in the Revelation symbolized understanding of John's own emotions from past lives, his seven spiritual centers, where memory of past lives dwells, his physical bodily needs, and his relationship to spiritual forces; and he was told to apply those understandings in his own life by eating the book.

Jean didn't eat the notebook, but it was placed in the light of the earth, or perhaps we should say the light of the world, and cleansed. The notebook for her was also a symbol of what she had done in the past, because she always wrote in it, and when it got dirty, she would discard the notebook, because of unconscious guilt. The cleansing meant for her that all that was done in the past has been washed away, in a sense—cleansed, forgotten. The slate is clean! Isn't that what we call forgiveness?

Throughout the world today, more and more individuals are experiencing the presence of the Christ, either in dreams, visions, or in meditation. And the encounter often is associated with the healing of an emotion, a memory, or a relationship—signifying an awakening, a healing within the one experiencing the event.

Healing today must be recognized as a life process, and as a movement in consciousness, from where one stands at the moment, toward his eventual destiny. Any illness and subsequent healing of the body can truly be as monumental an event in one's life as the vision Paul had while losing his sight on the road to Damascus. So we are alerted to the need of finding the gift, the opportunity, in any illness or accident, as we make our way through life.

We must also always keep in mind that meditation, or healing, or opening one's consciousness—any of these come about through attuning the physical and mental to the spiritual source. The spirit is there first, of course, and the spirit, being primary, does not need healing. It will act, irrespective of what we do about any of the factors existing in our physical or mental selves.

That is probably the key to understanding how spiritual healing comes about. The spirit will act, but what direction have we given it? How will we direct this Life Force that flows through our beings?

The ideal is perhaps best chosen to be the guiding light, the star in the distance, the light that the pilgrim keeps in sight, to make it possible to bring healing to another or to ourselves, if we would be a force for good in the earth. The mind is like the skipper tending the rudder on the boat—he guides and keeps us going in the direction we have chosen. The ideal is the direction we wish to take. In spiritual terms, the ideal is the Christ consciousness within, that which guides us into oneness with the Father. Cayce commented on ideals:

> Build . . .rather [upon] those that are as eternal influences in thy experiences; and these will bring harmony where there have been turmoils heretofore.
>
> Find thy ideals in spiritual things—then those in the mental and material will be the result. *2284-1*

Let's build then toward

> that for which each soul enters—to be a channel, to live to the highest ideal that is the concept of the individual.
>
> Keep the faith in self and in thy abilities, but keep them in accord with thy ideals in spiritual things. *2296-1*

There is no healing method that works all the time, of course. And spiritual healing follows this rule. It cannot be universally effective, if healing is an event in consciousness, an awakening to the Divine of forces within the body. And that is how we have defined it thus far.

It appears that the desire to heal activates a force within the healer which can be given or sent to another who is in need. The manner in which it is offered apparently is not the most important matter. The manner in which it is done is individual to the healer. The force is the same, whether it is channeled directly through the individual to the one who receives, or whether it activates abilities in the healer who then offers it as a healing energy. But it must produce an awakening, and that is the responsibility of the one in need.

The pattern of energies present within the body of the receiver of healing energies must be altered in order for there to be a restoration to normal. This involves the atoms. And we must recall once more that atoms are really energy.

A group of more than twenty-five people, all interested in this subject of spiritual healing, met with Edgar Cayce in June 1935 and asked him to give a reading on this subject. It is difficult to paraphrase what comes from a source such as this, so a portion of his reading is reproduced here as he gave it:

As we have indicated, the body-physical is an atomic structure subject to the laws of its environment, its heredity, its soul development.

The activity of healing, then, is to create or make a balance in the necessary units of the influence or force that is set in motion as the body in the material form through the motivative force of spiritual activity, sets in motion.

It is seen that each atom, each corpuscle, has within same the whole form of the universe—within its own structure.

As for the physical body, this is made up of the elements of the various natures that keep same in its motion necessary for sustaining its equilibrium; as begun from its (the individual body's) first cause.

If in the atomic forces there becomes an over-balancing, an injury, a happening, an accident, there are certain atomic forces destroyed or others increased; that to the physical body become either such as to add to or take from *the elan vital that makes for the motivative forces through that particular or individual activity.*

Then, in meeting these it becomes necessary for the creating of that influence within each individual body to bring a balance necessary for its continued activity about each of the atomic centers in its own rotary or creative force, its own elements for the ability of resuscitating, revivifying, such influence or force in the body.

How, then, does the activity of any influence act upon the individual system for bringing healing in the wake or the consciousness, to become conscious of its desire?

When a body, separate from that one ill, then, has so attuned or raised its own vibrations sufficiently, it may—by the motion of the spoken word— awaken the activity of the emotions to such an extent as to revivify, resuscitate or to change the rotary force or influence or the atomic forces in the activity of the structural portion, or the vital forces of a body, in such a way and manner as to set it again in motion.

Thus does spiritual or psychic influence of body upon body bring healing to any individual; where another body may raise that necessary influence in the hormone of the circulatory forces as to take from that within itself to revivify or resuscitate disease, disordered or distressed conditions within a body.

For, as has been said oft, any manner in which healing comes— whether by the laying on of hands, prayer, by a look, by the application of any mechanical influence or any of those forces, in materia medica— must be of such a nature as to produce that necessary within those forces about the atomic centers of a given body for it to bring resuscitating or healing.

The law, then, is compliance with the universal spiritual influence that awakens any atomic center to the necessity of its concurrent activity in relationships to other pathological forces or influences within a given body. Whether this is by spiritual forces, by any of the mechanical forces, it is of necessity one and the same. [281-24]

It's meeting problems at an atomic level, isn't it? And, when a healer works on one who is ill, with the word or the touch or whatever, it is to change the "rotary" forces or the atomic forces in such a manner as to bring improvement.

When one heals oneself, on the other hand, there are ways available (through hormones?) to take from within oneself those forces needed for rebuilding or healing.

The spiritual healing might then best be defined as an energy healing. But the energy always comes from the One Source. This, we must always remember.

CHAPTER 17

The Keys to Well-Being

Let's look at this search from a different perspective as we review how far we have come. Let's suppose that Edgar Cayce was right when he said that we were all created in the image of God before the world came into being, that we are spiritual beings on a journey through the earth, time after time, to regain the oneness with God that we had before we got lost, somehow, in the spiritual dimension where we originated.

Maybe we got lost because we rebelled and wanted to do our own thing. God couldn't stop us because he gave us free will, as well as life itself.

So we came into the earth, which was established for our benefit. But still there dwells inside ourselves the essence of our original creation, as well as the essence of the rebellion that we brought along with us. Therein lies the source of our difficulties in the earth, for our wars between our higher selves and our rebellious natures have brought disturbance and dis-ease into our lives.

And the implication, then, is that our existence in the earth is a time where we can find our way back to the Creator by letting go of the rebellion, the dis-ease, the disturbance, and creating healing and peace in its place.

That means, strange as it may seem, that we are—to one extent or another—all ill. So, what is illness, then? It can be defined in a number of ways, these being simply a very few:

- Lack of oneness of body, mind, and spirit.
- Lack of perfect emotional balance.
- Lack of perfect physiological function.
- Lack of perfect health.
- Lack of perfect love.
- Lack of that oneness that Jesus had with God and wanted us to experience.

We are all, then, in need of healing of the body, the mind, and the spirit. For our destiny, according to these readings, is oneness with God. We are eternal beings.

Our goal is not perfection, although that may be our eventual destiny. But we do aspire to a homeostasis—a dynamic equilibrium—of the body which we experience as "health." We would like to have a better emotional balance, be able to react in a loving way, find the joy that comes with simply feeling good and knowing that there is nothing significantly wrong with our bodies. This must be understood as a reasonable goal!

So how do we find it? Let's look at some of the keys involved in the search. Keys open doors, allow us entrance into other realms of consciousness. If we know what the keys are, then we will know how to make our journey and how to make the steps up the ladder to health more successful.

I'm quite sure, however, that if I were to give you the keys that are on my key chain, they would not fit your house, your car, your office, your storage shed, or whatever you have locked up. Keys are just not like that. We have already established that every human being is different, unique, and quite wonderful in so many ways. Our ability to choose in a variety of ways has already made that difference so real. And it certainly is well that we are all special in our own eyes and in the eyes of those we contact day by day.

The keys that might aid in opening certain doors in your search for healing would have to be those concepts or ideas that would keep you centered or grounded as they then guide you to take measured steps in your journey up the ladder to health. Let's make a list of important keys as they seem to have evolved out of the Cayce readings and in my experience. Then we can look at how some of them have been meaningful in people's lives.

1. *Always keep hope alive.* No illness or condition of the body is hopeless. Hope is tied in closely with faith, and faith often brings results that are totally unexpected and wonderful. So keep on hoping for what you are searching for.

2. *All illness can be overcome,* and all conditions of the body can be returned back to normal. Cayce once said that you can heal most any condition, but you can't heal a hard-headed, stiff-necked old man. He could have extended the adjectives to the female sex as well, I think. But healing can come about, *if* the attitude is right, and the individual needs a right attitude more than anything else.

3. *Always keep an open mind.* You never know when God is letting you in on a secret that may give you the healing that you are seeking. God speaks through children, loved ones, and even one's "enemies." And don't forget that enemies may only be mirrors for you or a puppet graciously giving you a life lesson on emotions or attitudes.

4. *Always choose constructively* insofar as your direction or your activity is concerned. Choice is such a powerful tool that it can destroy health as well as enhance it or bring it about. Use your power of choice as a golden key. Choose which way to go and then move on it. Never regret a choice you honestly made. It will always bring change and often unexpected opportunities for further choices. Life is like that. Change is always a necessity for growth. And healing is always growth. Allow yourself to adopt new ways of looking at things, new ways of doing things. Change by choice instead of being forced to change. The latter brings disease and depresses the state of health.

5. *Mind is the builder.* Be alert as to what your mind is doing. If

you say something or think something that is negative, remember that your body is obedient to that direction of the mind, so affirm something positive. Be ready to ask yourself about the statement that you made or thought. Is that an affirmation? If it was not recognized as an affirmation by your conscious mind, that doesn't stop your unconscious from accepting it and making it a rule of the body, whether positive or negative.

6. *Patience, persistence, and consistency* are as golden rules for bringing about healing of the body. These three spiritual qualities need to be worn as a cloak when seeking to heal the body.

7. *Normal assimilation and elimination* are essential to health.

8. *Keep an alkaline balance in the immune system.* The slightly higher pH than found in the bloodstream is necessary for protection and for healing and regeneration.

9. *In the midst of this "material" universe, remember your origin.* It's so easy to look around and see this beautiful world and think, "I'm really a part of this." Rather, our destiny lies in a domain far beyond our wildest imagination. On any kind of day, clear or cloudy, you can really see forever. It's not only where you came from, but your destiny. You are greater than you think.

10. *Find joy in all that you do.* If someone gets angry with you, be joyful that you can understand him and bless him. You certainly cannot control him. If your cat wakes you up in the middle of the night, don't kick him out of your bed, instead laugh about how cute he is, and turn over in bed and resume your dreaming. Laughter is healing for the body and a pleasure to the soul.

11. *Always look for guidance.* It can come in dreams, in symbols in the outside world, during meditation, through intuition or hunches, or in the still small voice. And we need the help that comes in this way. It strengthens us and aids us in our direction and choices.

12. *Above all, keep active!* Don't hesitate in your movements in this earth. In football, you would be tackled. In boxing, you'd be knocked out. In life, you will end up befuddled and indecisive. Do something, even if it's wrong. That way, you will always get an-

other chance. If it's right, you'll be that much more enlightened on your path. But, be sure you're using your other keys. That's the direction to health.

In helping others to move successfully toward health, I would again define true healing as the return to "normal" of body, mind, and spirit. This norm is a close parallel to that manner or form in which we were created. It might be thought of as a pattern or a blueprint of what we want to be, as we search deeply within ourselves for a goal or an ideal.

Part of my morning exercises is a twenty-five-minute ride on my stationary bicycle. I like to use that time creatively, so inside myself I call together all those angels, the forces or beings who have a consciousness of their own and who are at work constantly to keep me healthy. That is, if I let them keep me healthy—for sometimes the cares of the world take away my concentration and we—those beings, angels, or forces for good and I—don't get our conference completed early on in my bike-riding experience.

But when we are successful, I gather them together around the table in our conference room and let them know that they, like I, were brought into being by a beneficent being that we call the Creator, God, and that part of their job inside my body is to work to restore it back to normal. In order that they understand what I mean, I then tell them that we are going to look once more at the blueprint of the area they are working on, and refresh their minds so their work will be more productive.

At that point in the conference, I have them watch while this brilliant light form drifts down onto the table and changes from a three-dimensional form into a very complex but accurate picture of my body, much like a very professional blueprint. Then the blueprint scatters, like magic, to each of those beings that have charge of specific portions of my body.

Then they are instructed to look at their particular portion of the blueprint and really study what they are to do today. At that point, I dismiss them so they can go back to work, and then I encourage them, as I ride my bike, with visualization and words—telling them to normalize or to build or strengthen the body where it seems to me that my body does need attention.

This little exercise incorporates within it many of the concepts that it has been my privilege to learn from the Cayce material, as I've studied and worked with it over the nearly four decades since I was first introduced to this information. And so much of this material has been a part of my life in working with those individuals who are ill or preparing to become ill, even though they may not really notice the beginning of a disease.

Always try to recall that you are God's greatest creation in the universe. You were brought into being as an image of the God-Force. You have within your being all the potential that God has. You are eternal, in the sense that you will never cease being you.

So is it not realistic, then, to say that you are a spiritual being, that you came into existence before the world was formed, and you will still be in existence when the earth is rolled away as a scroll, to be no more.

You have the power to choose what you will do, and you have been doing this since before you first incarnated into the earth. For you, like the rest of us here on the earth, chose to move away from God and exercise your own powers. Now, you are on an adventure in consciousness trying to find your way back home, to where you started, in attunement with the Creative Forces of the Universe.

This is what we might call a thumbnail sketch of you and your heritage, and the destiny you can look forward to. So, we might ask, if we are nearly 5 billion years old by earth time, then is the so-called aging process a "normal" occurrence? For most of us have been conditioned by generations of forebears to think of ourselves getting older as we pass the thirties and forties, and retire to die when we get to be sixty-five.

This has an impact on healing, for our body tends to follow the suggestions given it from the mind, and if we think we are going to get old, we certainly will. So we need to recall to our minds what we really are and what our origin and destiny are, no matter how many incarnations we will or have experienced here in the earth. Planting that belief pattern into our unconscious mind helps to make of our bodies true believers about the fact that we are as young as we believe we are.

One of our geriatric patients was asked by a nurse, "How old are you?" His reply was "My age is none of my business!"—and he added after that, "And none of yours either!" He didn't believe in getting older. He was—and is—eternal.

Diseases of the elderly do not occur because the person is getting older. Many of those in the medical field might disagree with me in taking this position, but they may simply not have faced the concept that we are different from what we think we are. And we can live a long time. We discussed this business of longevity earlier in the book. Cayce suggested in many readings that longevity results when one maintains a balance of the bodily functions, a condition that creates that state of being we call "health"—and people generally don't die of good health.

Some years ago, a Yale doctor, Theodore Linz, reported on a seventy-six-year-old patient who had been hospitalized for heart failure and seemed completely disoriented. After the heart condition had been brought under control, the patient seemed to be oriented and rational. However, because this man of seventy-six kept saying that as soon as he was ready to go home his mother would drive over and pick him up, his physicians decided they had better keep him hospitalized for a few more weeks to see if they could further improve his mental state. "Then," says Dr. Linz, "one day his mother of ninety-five drove over from a town a hundred miles away, accompanied by her ninety-seven-year-old sister, and they took their little boy home." This story is found in Lawrence Galton's book *Don't Give Up on an Aging Patient* (Crown, 1975).

Many factors are involved in longevity, and these same principles are part of the strength or weakness in the process of healing the body. But the one thing that needs always to be kept in mind is our true nature, our true origin, and our ultimate destiny. And we need to put into the formula that we truly accept ourselves where we are today, but always looking to the future for growth that will bring us closer to our goal.

If one is to choose the fruits of the spirit as a purpose, an aim, or an ideal, the path becomes easier. As was discussed earlier in the book, there are two ways to learn, and we all must learn how to love. One way is the manner we took in the beginning when we rebelled and left the presence of God, and got lost. That's the hard way. When we are in rebellion, we do not learn by listening and believing. That is God's gentle way of instructing us as we wend our way, reincarnating through all these nations and races that populate the earth. When we won't listen, there is another way, the hard way. My granddad used to call it the school of hard knocks. In the world today, it is sometimes called karma.

Choosing the gentle way, the fruits of the Spirit, is what some call Grace. For all God wants is that we learn the important lessons in life. And these are lumped together and called "How to love one another." If we don't learn the easy way, we get the opportunity to learn the hard way. We each get to choose.

In the process of searching for healing of the body, we automatically take action. We have to ask others for help. We have to move this body of ours consciously in order to search. We may need to do some reading, attend classes, go somewhere. Action is not only needed, it is mandatory.

For me, I've learned that simply knowing something is of little value unless it is put to action in my life. Gaining much knowledge, looking for multiple ways of healing the body is just a wasteland in the mind, unless we take action. So, for me, action is a primary goal. And the only time we have is now—this moment! The only time in which we can act. Opportunities are lost by waiting.

In the Old Testament, Elijah was accosted by a widow woman (1 Kings 17:17–24) who had little to do with him because her son lay dead and she thought Elijah was come to call her sin to remembrance and to slay her son. Elijah was a man of action. He took the boy up into the loft where he was staying and laid him on his own bed. "He stretched himself upon the child three times, and cried unto the Lord, and said, 'O Lord my God, I pray thee, let this child's soul come into him again.' And the Lord heard the voice of Elijah; and the soul of the child came into him again, and he revived."

Elijah was a man of action. He believed what God had told him to do, and he did it. In the New Testament, there are numerous instances where Jesus knew what individuals needed to be healed. He spoke the word, and a man rose from the dead. It needed action, even though it was only speaking a word. Peter was a man of action always and was called the rock upon which the church would be founded.

To bring healing to ourselves, we must, in this dimension, follow our beliefs and ideals and make them active in our lives. Most often, it is necessary when we find ourselves in a situation where it hurts or it is uncomfortable. And that is always when we are in a relationship with another human being and one finds it necessary to love—with all that love means—or to fail in living out our belief. Healing often depends on just that.

We must also be in search of guidance, signs, and dreams, which can come in the most unexpected forms. Suppose, for instance, you are in your car, and you turn the key in the ignition and the car starts. You ask your very wise friend who is sitting in the passenger seat if he can give you some guidance as to where you ought to go. However, you are still parked alongside the curb. He says to you, "If you will move your car out from the curb, into traffic, I can help. But, until you are moving, you cannot be guided."

So we need to be moving, and the guidance will come if we ask for it. The most important direction will most often be found within one's own body, for we have been told that the kingdom of heaven is within. And, as we meditate in our inner selves, the answers will come as to what, where, and how we should measure our steps day by day. And justice, mercy, peace, and harmony are the gifts we receive from God when we seek his face. When we are looking for health guidance, it is well also to remember this short quote from Cayce:

> *The physician needed most is within self. The physician is the Christ Con-*
> *sciousness. Do not trust in forces other than those that are within self. Re-*
> *member, thy body is the temple of the living God. And He promises to meet*
> *you, as you attune yourself by the outer circulation. Ye can by the will of self*
> *make self in accord. Do it. Live it. Be it.* 3384-1

Meditation, quite simply described, is the technique of attuning the physical and the mental bodies to their spiritual source. Generally, the procedure is to sit with the spine straight and the feet flat on the floor. The eyes are closed and the head erect. The mind is quieted by centering itself on an affirmation, such as "Our Father, through the love that Thou hast manifested in the world through Thy Son, the Christ, make us more aware of 'God is Love.'"

Music is often used to help prepare one for meditation, and incense if desired. As you enter into the silence, the body is gradually stilled, then the mind. The mind is more difficult and you might find yourself thinking actively about most anything. The mind is quieted by returning to the affirmation and keeping it in one's mind's eye.

Often in meditation one will enter an expanded state of consciousness, and the guidance that one is seeking will often be found there, in the silence. Or it might come when the period of meditation is over. Ask and ye shall receive is the promise.

Sometimes the guidance will come before a particular meditation period. My wife, Peggy, and I went into our meditation room as usual one morning to begin meditation. There was nothing strange about the day or our lives that marked a difference. I lit our candle and then we both noticed at the same time that there was water on the open Bible that we always keep on the table between our two chairs. It was as if one or two teaspoons of water had been spilled on the open page. Only the left page was wet. It had not soaked through to the sheet behind it. We blotted it off at once, but the page remains a crinkled sheet, obviously the result of being wet. There is no source of water in that room. Both of us had taken a shower earlier, but were dried off and dressed when we went into our meditation room. No water came from the dry ceiling—it wasn't raining outside and had not rained for weeks here in Arizona. And we had not been carrying water around in any fashion.

The Bible was opened to the book of John. It was John, of course, who was the youngest among the four apostles, and a true mystic. It was he who also wrote the supernatural and symbolic book *The Revelation of St. John, the Divine*. The page that was affected was the fourth chapter of the Gospel According to Saint John, in which he talked about Jesus at Jacob's well. Jesus had asked the Samaritan woman who had come to draw water if she would give him water to drink, since his disciples had gone to the city to buy some meat. "Then saith the woman of Samaria unto him, 'How is it that thou, being a Jew askest drink of me, which am a woman of Samaria? For the Jews have no dealings with the Samaritans.'

"Jesus answered and said unto her, 'If thou knewest the gift of God, and who it is that saith to her, "Give me to drink"; thou wouldest have asked of him, and he would have given thee living water.' The woman saith unto him, 'Sir, thou hast nothing to draw with, and the well is deep; from whence then has thou that living water? Art thou greater than our father Jacob, which gave us the well, and drank thereof himself, and his children, and his cattle?'

"Jesus answered and said unto her, 'Whosoever drinketh of this water shall thirst again: But whosoever drinketh of the water that I shall give him shall never thirst; but the water that I shall give him shall be in him a well of water springing up into everlasting Life'" (John 4:7–14).

You can read the rest of the story, but it had a deep impact on both my wife and me. We have committed ourselves to work with the Cayce information at the A.R.E. Clinic and to serve God through that work. Our writing and our teaching is a product of that commitment. The water that came out of the ethers through an unrecognized medium was calling us to attention, saying, "This is your well of water as it is in every person's life, if you will accept it. Study its deeper meaning, for you, like every other inhabitant of this globe, were fashioned as an eternal being in the image of that Force that created the universe itself."

Guidance can come also from signs. Not only the kind of signs like the Biblical sign of Jonah, when he was swallowed by a whale. But in modern times, helpful bits of information about your health can come from seeing a sign on the side of a commercial vehicle, from simply observing what is happening around you, from listening to what is being said by family or friend, or from observing what is happening in nature. It is a learning process.

My experience of traveling eighty miles an hour through the California desert on a hot July afternoon, then having one of my tires blow out in the city limits of Wickenburg taught me a lesson. It was a sign! I learned—at a meaningful level—that there really are angels who watch over and care for me. That tire was worn clear through, with seven holes in the casing showing the inner tube inside. It has boggled my mind a bit, visualizing those angels flying around, keeping a hand over those holes and keeping the tire from exploding long before it did. And leaving me in a town where I could get a replacement.

I'm sure the angels are helping me, too, when I deal with health or healing episodes in my own body or in those who consult with me about their health. We are given guidance even when we are not aware of it. Every individual has a guardian angel who supervises how little or how much trouble is to be avoided. Children especially need this kind of help.

The most prolific source for guidance, however, comes through dreams. One of my close friends had a dream in which he went down into his cellar (he lived in a one-story house at the time, with no cellar) and inspected the plumbing. It was not working right, seemed to be partially plugged at one point. The dream seemed to him to be talking about his body's elimination system, the lower part, and that it was plugged up.

Knowing the importance of elimination in the care of his body, he scheduled himself for a colonic the next day, and he discovered that the dream had in fact told him about the condition of his lower bowel. He also dreamed that he had a large bunch of carrots on his plate at the dinner table. He had not been getting enough vegetables in his diet, and he especially avoided carrots.

Most dreams are not that clear, but when one is asking for guidance through dreams, his psychic abilities bring together information that can cross the barrier that usually exists between the conscious and the unconscious mind, and present him with a series of symbols that can be interpreted and that will answer the question being asked.

There are principles that govern every significant step we take toward healing. They are not grounded on scientific research, necessarily, but they are part of the Divine plan for the human body, and God has not given us the ability yet to fully understand the amazing nature of this electrical unit we call the body, or the energy that carries with it information and consciousness.

We find that we need to move always with our eventual goal in mind—that of becoming one with the Creative Forces of the Universe. We do it here a little, there a little, always being aware that there are reasons and principles underlying every step. We need to seek always for coordination, cooperation, and the awakening of the deeper areas of consciousness within ourselves.

Our climb up the ladder, then, helps the body to become healed, depending in part on what we do to aid that healing effort and cooperate with all the attempts that might be expended inside and outside the body.

We might think of that ladder as having twelve steps, or twelve rungs, which we need always to be sure are in good repair for our climb. These include:

1. Use our eating habits to build health.

We all have habits that rule most of our waking hours, and especially those times when we eat. There are well-known rules to healthy eating in these latter days of the twentieth century. We have the power of choice, but it will never do us any good unless it is used constructively about our eating. If we work at it, we can create new habits of eating that will build our bodies into a higher level of health. "Choose Thou!"

A basic diet for health would have lots of vegetables and fruits; fish or fowl for protein; avoid fried foods, white flour, and white sugar; and go very easy on desserts and all kinds of sweets.

2. Put knowledge, faith, and ideals into action.

Create an ideal for your life that you are willing to follow. Let it be something that is creative and constructive, never destructive or for the self alone. Identify for yourself what higher force you really believe in. Then act as if you have faith in that higher force that you will be guided and shown the way through your life, as well as through your search for healing. In other words, act as if these things are real in your life, and then *take action*.

3. Pray and meditate, and ask others to pray for you.

Why worry when you can pray? Cayce said, "Pray ye, then, that ye be ready in the hour of trial or temptation; that ye may say, even as He, 'Not my will but Thine, O God, be done in and through me; that I may have that estate with thee that was before the worlds were—and be conscious of same.'

"This ye may be aware of only as the whole trust of body, of mind, of soul, is put in Him . . .

"Thy body, indeed, then, is the temple of the living God. There Creation is manifested. Each morning is but another opportunity" (3188-1).

Then, when you have sought that oneness with God in prayer, ask those you love and those in your support group to pray for you. No prayer goes unanswered.

Meditation is attuning your physical and mental self to the Divine. It needs to be done regularly, and it is in that period that one may hear the still, small voice that will guide and direct your ways.

4. *Use castor oil packs and other Cayce remedies.*

Castor oil has a vibration that is cleansing and healing, no matter where it is applied. Called "The Oil That Heals," or the "Palma Christi," it always helps the immune system, like having the Palm of the Christ placed on your body. And it is well to remember that the immune system is the prime defender of body health and has an ability to rejuvenate and regenerate the body. When a castor oil pack is applied over the liver and the upper right part of the abdomen, the flow of the lymph and the ability to respond to any threat of the body is enhanced in the thymus and the rest of the immune system which it directs.

In using any of the Cayce remedies, visualize the effectiveness of the remedy to awaken the consciousness of the tissues inside the body to their spiritual source.

For more information refer to the A.R.E., Virginia Beach, VA.

5. *Exchange hugs and touches with regularity.*

When you hug people or touch them, you change their electromagnetic field, and what some call their aura. Give of yourself when you touch. Know, when you do this, that you are a channel through which the power of the Divine is always manifesting. The touch will bring that power without the use of words. Accept hugs and touches with the same attitude and thank the Giver.

6. *Exercise—move your body. Or have others work on your body.*

Walking, riding a bike, and swimming are said to be the best kinds of exercise. In any event, it's breaking a law if you do not move your body regularly. The penalty for breaking that law is that your body will stiffen up in those places where you have refused to exercise. You are here on the earth to *do* things. Exercises help to keep you in good health, so that you might fulfill your purpose in being born this time around.

If you don't get enough exercise, get someone else to move your body for you: osteopaths, chiropractors, physical massage therapists—even some medical doctors will give you a treatment.

They all have their specific methods and techniques, and they can do an excellent job. So care for your body—either move it regularly or get it moved regularly. Your body will indeed thank you for your attention.

7. *Work with your dreams.*

First, record your dreams. Your unconscious will not have a high regard for you if you don't. The dream guide part of your unconscious will think you are not being serious.

Dreams bring to your conscious awareness information from the totally unconscious part of yourself that helps to guide you, direct your path, and give you insights into your past.

Edgar Cayce said, "The dreams again and again present to the entity those lessons, those truths, that the entity seeks to apply in the life, and as these are presented may the entity take those warnings and those lessons from same, and applying same in the life bring about those things that bring more peace, more satisfaction, and a better understanding of the conditions, the purposes, and all of life—for it is not all of life to live, nor yet all of death to die" (136-62).

If you have a question that is very important—or even not so important—it is reasonable and helpful to ask it of your unconscious and get a truthful reply from your dreams.

8. *Take steps toward regeneration of your body.*

Electricity can help to make it happen. The Cayce readings repeatedly state that electricity or electronics is the nearest we can come to a manifestation of God in the earth. Not God, but the *manifestation* of God. And Cayce also described several energy-type devices that can aid in the healing of the body or in creating longevity.

Never forget that your body is a totally electrical organism. And the impulses flowing through your nervous system are of the nature of the Creative Forces. That's the flow of life itself.

If you want to live a long time, you'd better have something to do to help others. For that's what life is all about. The electricity—the life force itself—moving through our bodies offers us the help that we need. However, we all tend to distort the life force to our own desires. For longevity to happen, the nature of God, as love and gentleness, kindness, and so on, has to move through us and then outward to serve those whom we contact. With love.

9. *Eliminate what you don't need.*

Eliminate attitudes that are not helpful, excess contents of the intestinal tract, "things" in your life that clutter up your garage and storage areas.

Make sure you eliminate all those used and refused forces from your bloodstream into your digestive tract—they become a burden and a creator of ill health if you don't. In the same manner, let go of those hates, angers, animosities, conceits, criticisms, envies, disappointments, frustrations, worries, blames, and so on, that you have been nurturing for a

long time. Symbolically, cleaning out your closets and giving away some of those things that haven't been used for
years will help cleanse your whole system.

10. *Pick an attitude that will be helpful and practice it. Pick
    another.*

    Attitudes begin when they are chosen for the very first
    time, then become stronger when practiced as you move
    along your chosen path. They may be constructive or de-
    structive. Practice each of those attitudes that you say you
    believe should be part of you because they are so good,
    daily, until it becomes part of your personality and makes
    you, in the eyes of others (and yourself), a better and more
    beautiful person.

11. *Get help from a counselor in learning about yourself, one
    who sees things in the light of past lives and ultimate pur-
    poses.*

    We cannot see ourselves well without some kind of help. A
    counselor aids us by holding up a mirror for us to see. A
    spouse can seldom do that, because the spouse most often
    becomes the mirror and this kind of relationship engenders
    discord and misunderstandings. But get someone who
    knows how to help in the context of looking at each per-
    son as an eternal being who has been through many, many
    lifetimes, and is still learning. We all need this kind of help.

12. *Find a support group and let them help.*

    The A.R.E. Search for God study groups, for instance, pro-
    vide a good example. When you have been given advice
    about healing from whatever source, and you want to get
    some good, friendly, and insightful feedback, a group is
    very helpful. It's been in this kind of a format that thou-
    sands of individuals have learned how to work with their
    dreams, and how to offer helpful insights for other mem-

bers of the group. But there are also many illness-specific support groups across the world.

If you join a group, make strong efforts to keep going. It is that business of persistence and consistency again. Very important for success in any endeavor.

These twelve steps are not likely to be taken completely all at one time. This becomes too large a task. Remember that we have been here in the earth through many incarnations, learning habits here and there that become attitudes which really sometimes move us through life in ways that we may not approve of, until we search our conscience and higher awarenesses.

An undertaking to change all those attitudes in one fell swoop is not likely to succeed. So it becomes important to take what abilities we do have in hand and begin. I think it was wise for the Cayce readings to take the attitude of reminding us that a little leaven leavens the whole lump. It does happen a bit at a time— here a little, there a little, line upon line, precept upon precept.

As you move along these steps toward the top of the ladder, you will undoubtedly experience moments when you hear something you have heard before and didn't understand, but then, this moment, suddenly a light goes on and you all at once realize, "*That's* what it means!" These bits of wisdom are simply a gradual awakening of your heritage.

When we consider that we are intended to be co-creators with God, able to do and to know that which the Creator of the Universe knows and does, it becomes mind-boggling, and we have to stop for a while to consider, Is this where I am heading? Am I capable of all that?

Well, the Cayce story is that you are and you will be both knowing and doing what God has known and done. It is understandable that He knows we will be a while getting there, with efforts being interspersed with failures and difficulties. But the direction has to be taken and the movement has to be made. And if we recall that our "try" is held by God to be righteousness, then we can tolerate our missteps and at the same time gain in wisdom and growth toward our destiny. I've included a list of references at the back of the book that may be helpful for you in your adventure.

In Search of Healing

Our origin is our destiny. At the top of the ladder is a light. It shows us that what we have seen as our beginning is also what we have inherited as our destiny. We must come to know ourselves to be ourselves, yet one with those Creative Forces we call God, and in the midst of our journey. The light up here lets us understand better where we are. For we are certainly farther along than we were when we first entered the earth, though we still have a long way to go.

And somehow, we come to realize, the search for healing is a very integral part of our growth toward that goal that Edgar Cayce spoke of so many times: the oneness with God. For each time we are healed, we are given another piece of the puzzle, another gift in understanding ourselves and our relationship with our fellow human beings and with God. Still, our vision is not yet perfect, and some of the steps along the way are only dimly perceived in the distant reaches of time.

We were created as souls, and the soul is understood to be spirit, mind, and will. The heritage of the power to choose came about when creation occurred—if, indeed, there is the quality of time in that dimension. And it was by choice—the exercise of the will—that we were brought into the earth plane of existence. But the earth had to be created first, and the beauty of that happening was caught by the Cayce readings in a number of instances where questions were asked about the beginning of things.

If we are here to be of service to others, as Cayce suggests, then it seems that we are actually trying to heal ourselves, through making ourselves of service to our fellow man. And the healing is clearing away debris that may have accumulated over aeons of time. Each step we take makes the load a bit lighter, and leads us more out of the darkness into the light. It may be the process we are going through in learning how to love. That in itself may be the healing secret. We have been told about it over those same aeons of time, but we are slow about putting it to the test.

The nature of the spiritual quest is the attunement of the physical and mental bodies to their spiritual source. For, without the physical and the mental, the spirit would have no place to lodge. We are, indeed, one being, and need to take action in accord with that idea.

The seekers will recognize the path and will find this advice from the Cayce readings to be applicable in their experience of their search for healing of the body:

> Then may ye as seekers of the way, may ye that have come seeking to know, to experience, to FEEL that presence of the Christ Consciousness within thine own breast, within thine own experience,
>
> OPEN the door of thy heart! For He stands ready to enter, to those who will bid Him enter.
>
> He comes not unbidden, but as ye seek ye find; as ye knock it is opened. As ye live the life is the awareness of His closeness, of His presence, thine.
>
> Then, again as He gave, "Love ye one another," thus fulfilling ALL that is in the purpose of His entrance into materiality; to replace hate and jealousy and those things that make one afraid, with love and hope and joy. 5749-10

So, the light not only shows us the way, perhaps, and extends our understanding of that which was our beginning and where we are destined to go in the future, but it also gives us more understanding about how we came to be healthy or ill, how the physiology of our body can be influenced by myriad factors, and how the series of experiences and incarnations had its start in the first place.

It seems that God did indeed create you and me as souls in His image. He gave us life through what we call spirit, and fashioned inside that soul the power of the mind, and the greatest of His gifts, the will, the power to choose.

This brought us to the point of making that first entrance into this dimension we call the earth plane, and the story from there on has been recounted through the pages of this book. From the point of creation onward to the present, our experiences have involved the constant use and power of the will in choosing what we are becoming—whether we have been aware of that choice or not. And it is that same power that can lead us back.

Let's move onward from the present, in search of healing at an even deeper level, and let life and its wonders keep us up where the Light can be discovered, at the top of the ladder.

Suggested Reading

Attitudes and Emotions, The Edgar Cayce Readings, Volumes 13, 14, 15, Association for Research and Enlightenment, Inc., A.R.E. Press, Virginia Beach, VA, 1982.

Becker, Robert O., and Selden, Gary. *The Body Electric*, William Morrow and Company, Inc., 105 Madison Ave., New York, NY 10016, 1985.

Bro, Harmon Hartzell. *A Seer Out of Season: The Life of Edgar Cayce*, New American Library (Penguin Books USA Inc.), 1633 Broadway, New York, NY 10019, 1989.

Chopra, Deepak. *Ageless Body, Timeless Mind*, Crown Publishers, Inc., 201 E. 50th St., New York, NY 10022, 1993.

Church, W.H. *Many Happy Returns, The Lives of Edgar Cayce*, Harper and Row, San Francisco, CA, 1984.

Green, Elmer and Alice. *Beyond Biofeedback*, Knoll Publishing Co., Inc., 1977.

Jampolsky, Gerald G. *Good Bye to Guilt*, Bantam Books, 666 Fifth Ave., New York, NY 10103, 1985.

McGarey, William A. *The Edgar Cayce Remedies*, Bantam Books, 666 Fifth Ave., New York, NY 10103, 1983.

———. *The Oil That Heals*, A.R.E. Press, P.O. Box 656, Virginia Beach, VA 23451.

Pitskhelauria, Georgi A. *The Longliving of Soviet Georgia*, Human Sciences Press, 72 Fifth Ave., New York, NY 10011, 1982.

Reilly, Harold J. and Brod, Ruth Hagy. *The Edgar Cayce Handbook for*

Health Through Drugless Therapy, Macmillan Publishing Co. Inc., 866 Third Ave., New York, NY 10022.

Rusznyak, I., Foldi, M., Szabo, G. *Lymphatics and Lymph Circulation*, Pergamon Press, Ltd., London, 1967.

Sharma, I.C. *Cayce, Karma & Reincarnation*, Theosophical Publishing House, Wheaton, IL, 1975.

Smith, A. Robert. *Hugh Lynn Cayce: About My Father's Business*, The Donning Company, 5659 Virginia Beach Blvd., Norfolk, VA 23502, 1988.

Spalding, Baird T. *Life & Teaching of the Masters of the Far East*, Vols 1-5, Devorss & Co., Marina del Rey, CA 90291, 1927.

Thurston, Mark. *Discovering Your Soul's Purpose*, A.R.E. Press, P.O. Box 656, Virginia Beach, VA 23451, 1984.

Woodward, Mary Anne. *Scars of the Soul*, Brindabella Books, Rt. 1, Box 127, Fair Grove, MO 65648, 1985.

Yogananda, Paramahansa. *Autobiography of a Yogi*, Self-Realization Fellowship, Los Angeles, CA, 1946.

SOURCES FOR MORE INFORMATION

A.R.E. Clinic, Inc., 4018 N. 40th St., Phoenix, AZ 85018.

Association for Research and Enlightenment, Inc., P.O. Box 595, Virginia Beach, VA 23451.

About the Author

Dr. William McGarey is the author of ten books built on his forty years' experience in applying the concepts of healing found in the Edgar Cayce Readings to thousands of patients with amazingly helpful results.

Dr. McGarey believes there is a great need for the kind of health care that the Cayce approach makes possible for anyone. For it awakens our minds to the reality of our origins and our destiny, and calls for us to be active in helping others to awaken in the same manner, to be ready for changes that have been predicted for the earth and the consciousness of those who dwell here.